Fighting Back!

Vantage
Publishing

Vantage Publishing

Other Titles by George Boelcke:

Colorful Personalities: Discover your personality type through the power of Colors

Colorful Personalities – Audio CD

The Colors of Leadership and Management

Colors at Work

The Colors of Parent & Child Dynamics

The Colors of Relationships

Colors Tools for Christians

The Colors of Sales and Customers

The Colors of PFS Recruiting

(All available through: www.vantageseminars.com)

Life in Colors (Published by Kane Miller for Usborne Books)

It's Your Money! Tools, tips & tricks to borrow smarter and pay it off quicker (U.S. and Canadian Editions)

The American Financial Nightmare – Audio CD

¡Quédese con Su Dinero! Los Secretos del Crédito y la Deuda

(All available through: www.yourmoneybook.com)

Fighting Back!

*How to take back financial control,
restore your credit and reach your debt freedom*

George J. Boelcke, CCP

Vantage Publishing

Design, layout & typeset: Ingénieuse Productions, Edmonton
Edited by: Christina Heinze
Cover art assistance: Madison Rudman

FIRST EDITION
Printed and bound in the United States of America

National Library of Canadian Cataloguing in Publication

Boelcke, George J., 1959-, author
        Fighting back! : how to take back financial control, restore
your credit and reach your debt freedom / George J. Boelcke, CCP.

Includes index.
ISBN 978-0-9784570-5-1 (pbk.)

        1. Finance, Personal. 2. Consumer credit. I. Title.

        HG179.B63 2013   332.024   C2013-902216-3

This book is dedicated to:

You – for investing in yourself and in this book, and wanting to improve your current financial situation. Whether you think you can – or think you can't – you'll be right either way. Hopefully, you'll choose the former.

Anyone who uses these tools and insights to help others becomes debt free. In the words of Zig Ziglar: "You can have anything you want in life if you will help enough other people get what they want." Keep sharing these tools, keep growing, and keep making a difference. It will matter a lot – to a lot of people.

Contents

Introduction

I was pissed! It was 3 A.M. and I couldn't sleep, so I was checking my email. This had to be a mistake. There's no way this was correct. All I had to do was pick up the phone and this would be fixed. Or that's what I thought...

I have been very fortunate in my life. I had always believed I was the luckiest person on the face of the planet. And I still do. I believe there's a positive in everything that gets thrown at you. I have been blessed with a dream wife, four awesome kids, and have done very well financially. I had grown up in a trailer park in western Kansas, accumulated only 27 credit hours after 2-1/2 years of full-time college, yet by 29, I had been named one of the Top 10 Young Entrepreneurs in North America.

... The email alert said that my credit score had changed. I logged in and checked – it had dropped more than 100 points! Why? What catastrophe had happened to cause this? Had someone stolen my identity and run-up hundreds of thousands of dollars of charges? Nope. A collection agency claimed I defaulted on a $143 bill.

WHAT? I had been making over a million dollars a year since age 30. I had never defaulted on anything in my entire life! It was 3 A.M., so I had to wait another five hours to talk to a live person. When I finally did, the person at the collection agency said I could pay them the $143 and they would report that it had been paid, but the default would not be removed from my credit report. It was as if they were holding my credit score for ransom, for 143 bucks that wasn't even legitimate!

By the end of the process I realized that's exactly what they were doing. And it wasn't just me, but millions of others. After a few hours on the phone, and doing a few hours of research, it turned out that this was a mistake by a cell phone company that wasn't even in business anymore. It took me more than 100 hours and several months of writing emails, making phone calls, and getting passed from one person to another before my destroyed credit score was finally restored.

It was obvious to me that most people would have given up far before I had and paid the $143 ransom. But the damage to their credit scores would have cost them tens of thousands of dollars in higher rates for years to come, plus countless headaches in other areas that most people aren't even aware of!

It was as if the banks, credit card companies, credit reporting agencies, and collection agencies were conspiring against the American people to increase their own profits. And THAT'S EXACTLY WHAT MANY ARE DOING! I knew right then and there: it was time to start fighting back!

In 2009 I decided I was going to do whatever it took to stop this from happening to millions of other Americans. Debt, and all the industries associated with it, is the biggest problem facing our country today. It's also one of the biggest problems many individuals face.

This industry is NEVER going to fix itself. Politicians are NOT going to fix it. The only way it will get fixed is to start a grassroots movement, beginning with you and me: We the People – will stand up and fight back – first for ourselves – and then for others. This book was conceived to help you, and to arm you for that movement.

If each of us just raised our credit score by 30 points, we'd save over $20 billion a year in interest. If you did just two or three simple steps to increase your credit score, the rate on your new mortgage loan, new credit card, next car financing, and even your insurance would drop a TON. But which companies would want you to do that? NONE! Because every company, and all of those industries, make MORE money when you're uninformed and don't know how to fight back. The less you know about the inside world of credit – the more THEY make, and the more YOU lose!

When I started to fight back, my first call was to financial author, radio personality, and personal friend George Boelcke. I asked him to write a book that would arm all of us with the tools we would need to gain the knowledge and confidence to fight back. I had read his book *It's Your Money!* and was impressed with how he was able to make financial insights so simple to understand and to implement.

I really value his honest, in your face, and tell it like it is style. His first response was 'no'. He had written over a dozen bestsellers on personality types, team building, sales, leadership, and building better relationships. He was already traveling all over the world impacting thousands of people in positive ways. I didn't really hear the word 'no'. I seldom do… I just heard 'not yet'.

George has a credit management degree and has spent over 20 years in finance and credit. He has never done any paid endorsements and has never taken a dime from anyone for any plug, promotion, or ad. He did agree to do some research and help me get traction on this critical crusade. The more we talked, and the more research George did, the more he understood my urgency for fighting back – the need for this book.

It's a simple, in your face, tell like it is, how to get debt free book. He exposes the major players and culprits who keep you in debt your entire life, and tells you exactly what to do, and what to avoid. I personally challenge you to get yourself debt free and pay it forward by helping others to do the same.

Thank you, George. Your book will change and empower countless lives. God is proud of you.

Shane Rudman
Proverbs 3: 5&6

PS: HEY YOU! Yes, you, reading this right now… I prayed for you to see this message. I believe you were born special. You're supposed to do something great with your life. This is your sign. Now join me and GO DO IT!

To fight back, you'll need to get
off the cruise ship and onto the battleship.

Can I Ask You a Question?

*You're always free to make any financial choices you wish,
but you're never exempt from the consequences.*

Would you come on the radio with me for an interview about the state of your financial situation? If you're like most people, there isn't a chance you'd agree to that. But why? Aren't you proud of the way you handle your money, spending, and borrowing?

The first interview question would be regarding how much money you've earned so far since you've left school. If you've worked for 10 years, even with $30,000 in income a year, that's $300,000 you've earned so far. What do you have to show for it in savings? How much do you have in an emergency account? How much money is coming off your check for retirement savings, or how much are you paying yourself each month? How would you handle a $2,000 emergency today, or what's your plan if you were to miss one paycheck?

What's the balance and interest rate on your credit card, and when was the last time it was paid in full? Can you show me your monthly budget and your last free credit bureau report? What's your approximate credit score, and what are the next two steps you're working on in order to raise it?

If you're in a relationship, what are the financial goals you and your partner have for the next two years, 10-years, and for retirement? How much term life insurance do you have? How long do you two go without having an argument or fight about money?

Those are just some basic and simple questions, yet they are so critical. If you'd rather not answer them in a radio interview, have you ever asked them of yourself? Money certainly does talk.

Unfortunately, for most people, it just says goodbye. If something is important enough, you'll always find a way. If it's not, you'll always find an excuse. Hopefully, you'll want to turn things around to do more of what works and less of what doesn't. But, since 80% of high school students never get a course on credit and finances, you and most other adults don't know the questions to ask, the pitfalls to avoid, the consequences of bad borrowing choices, or the financial tools to do more of what works and less of what doesn't.

Knowledge really is power. In the new financial reality of tighter credit and increased regulations, you have to know that the big banks, investment firms, brokers, and lenders will find other innovative ways to make money. And it'll always be at your expense if you don't have the tools and insights to make the right decisions and to protect yourself.

For these institutions, it's back to business as usual. They took nothing more than a two-year setback thanks to your bailouts. To them, the financial pain and suffering they inflicted was nothing they believed they were even accountable for. In the words of Goldman Sachs' CEO to the Times of London, the company was just "doing God's work." I'm a Christian, and what these investment firms, the big banks, and a ton of mortgage brokers did is nothing that God would condone!

As a result, you need to keep growing – keep asking questions. Always get a second opinion and a third quote, and perhaps read some of the chapters for the fourth time before you act. It's worth it – you're worth it. It might not be easy to change your financial situation around, but then, most things worth having aren't easy, or they wouldn't be so worth it.

To your credit,
George Boelcke, CCP

Why You Need to Know

*The price of getting financially informed is significantly
less than the cost of your financial mistakes.*

Credit – love it or hate it – almost everyone uses it and most people can't live without it. Unfortunately, most people also don't understand it very well and that costs dearly in the added interest you may pay and total debt you can accumulate over time.

This book should become your best friend. It is an invaluable resource for having a basic understanding of credit – for getting it, keeping it, and getting rid of it as fast as possible. Plus, it'll help you to understand your options. People who are uninformed, in a hurry, unwilling to ask questions, or are easily intimidated, will never obtain the best deal for themselves. Let's face it; nobody else has a vested interest in explaining shortcuts, savings, or options to you.

Every day, countless numbers of consumers make poor or uninformed credit decisions that create consequences for years to come. It's never by choice; it's because they don't know the credit tricks or pitfalls, or the right questions to ask first.

How did you and so many other people get here, and how do you avoid some of these expensive traps? It will be through understanding the inside rules and tips of credit – how to get it in the least costly way. It is also through managing debt – the how to get rid of it part.

Obtaining credit isn't a gift or a windfall as it only creates spending power for today. The downside is that you have to repay the money at some point. That's spending more money later when interest charges are added to make up for the gotta have it today purchase, is what will get you into trouble every time.

When you're making payments on last year's stuff,
you're using up a lot of money that can't be
saved or put toward this year's stuff.

Your current financial reality came about from a series of choices, conscious or unconscious choices. If you don't like where you're at, you will need to make different choices. Hopefully you'll make them based on wanting to become debt free and financially independent. If you're just going to do what's easy, life is going to be very hard. But if you're prepared to do what's hard, for just a few years, life will become really easy.

Have you ever been debt free? If you're like the vast majority of people, that hasn't happened since the day you started college or moved out of your parents' home. But, imagine what would it feel like if you were debt free? Peaceful, satisfied, blessed, stress-free, rich, self-confident, relaxed, happy, proud, content? What are your adjectives that come to mind if you choose to be (yes, it's entirely your choice) debt free?

Conversely, staying in debt and having your entire paycheck wiped out to make every lender rich while having little to nothing to show for it, also creates feelings. Sooner or later, these feelings will get stronger and harder to ignore. Stressed, broke, desperate, helpless, locked in, trapped, can't breathe, fearful, ashamed, angry, overwhelmed, or out of control? Read the list again and then decide which one you would rather have, or how you would want to live your life. Then take the steps you know you need to take in order to actually get much more of what you want – if you just take the two or three years to get there. Can you do it? Of course! Will you do it? That's up to you.

"Worry is the interest paid by those who borrow trouble."
George Washington

At the height of 2007 and 2008, 75% of the US economy was driven by consumer spending – your spending. There has never been another country where consumer spending had been that high. If you were a retailer, those years were great while they lasted. However, as an individual, that merry go round couldn't last forever. At one point, spending reached 137% of incomes. There were a ton of phony on-paper-only rich people living on credit cards, HELOCs, and interest-only mortgages sold to them by businesses and industries that made a fortune helping people become broke. Borrowing over and over again to keep up with current obligations was and will always be a suicidal pyramid scheme. For governments, just as much for individuals, it's a recipe for financial disaster that will always come to an end sooner rather than later.

> *"We're (still) heading for a financial cliff… but then, I can tell you that's because I'm not running for office…"*
> Ali Velshi – Host of CNN's Your Money

Entire industries and businesses in the last 20 years were built on two false premises: selling stuff to people which they could not afford, and inventing financing with insane plans, subprime loans, don't pay for a year, or credit cards with limits more than a years' worth of income. Plus, vehicle finance plans and dealers would also give you $5,000 towards your credit cards, or cover that $6,000 shortfall on your current loan. They would offer you a no-money-down option, or other similar traps. It was mostly marketed by businesses ranging from being completely crooked to having questionable ethics at best; and offered to people who couldn't afford their last car, never mind the new one they bought!

Those businesses kept hiding their mismanagement, incompetence, and phony business models. The false representations made by the businesses had others think the growth in these businesses would go on forever. While these businesses took on unsustainable debt, most individuals did as well. Much of the economic growth until 2008 was smoke and mirrors, because it was built in large measure on borrowed money. Now the country has little of the economic growth and all the debt hangover from three trillion dollars consumers borrowed the decade prior. The last recession officially ended back in June 2009; but, for vast numbers of people things got way worse, and most still haven't fully recovered.

Even back between 2009 and 2011, consumer debt was reduced by over a trillion dollars, or roughly 10% (today it's approaching two trillion dollars). Yet, banks, governments, and economists thought that was a really bad idea. Why were all those people and institutions cheering for you to fail? Because the old reality was that 75% of the economy was based upon your spending! Hopefully, you're done with that. It was a great few years, but paying it back will take a whole lot longer. In the new financial reality, it becomes even more critical that you have the insights and knowledge about your finances, borrowing options, rights, and choices.

In the last 50 years, there have been eight recessions.
You can be sure that the last one was not the last one.
Hopefully before the next one you'll be debt-free
and well on your way to building wealth,
rather than still making payments.

Credit Bureaus: Your Entire Financial Life In One Report

Credit reports are the "de facto economic passport for every individual in this country, whether you like it or not."
TransUnion spokesperson testifying at an
Oregon Senate Committee hearing

Credit rating agencies, or credit bureaus, are clearing houses of information. The largest three that every lender uses are Equifax, TransUnion, and Experian. You, like everyone else, has a file with each of them. If you don't know them – they certainly know you. They have over 210 million files, sell about 3 billion reports a year, and update over 4.5 billion pieces of data each month.

Credit bureaus don't actively gather much of their information. They collect information from banks, credit card issuers, and almost all other lenders. They don't rate customers, but accumulate, sort and sell factual information as central clearinghouses. At regular intervals, tens of thousands of lenders simply exchange their data with the credit bureaus by computer, which instantly update your files with new accounts or fresh information.

Every lender uses the credit bureaus as a reference source. Lenders receive a reduced price to purchase files in return for exchanging their customer data. So you can stop wondering if your late payment won't be reported or if a repossession might not show up. It will – and quite quickly. After all, your credit rating is your factual, detailed financial reputation, and lenders and credit bureaus have much longer memories than debtors.

Why you need to know

If someone at work is running around trashing you behind your back, you'd want to know. After all, it's damaging your reputation, impacting your job, and could sabotage a promotion or a raise. However, that's just one person doing it. When it comes to your credit file, everybody gets to know the information, no matter how wrong or outdated, and they don't take anything else into consideration but your credit report and credit score.

Only the information in your credit file makes up your credit score. If your file is incomplete or inaccurate, it'll cause your credit score to drop, and that number is used by large parts of the world to make vast numbers of decisions about you. (See the credit scoring chapter). The time to find out that there is inaccurate information is not the day after you've been turned down for credit. At that point, it'll take two or three months to fix the error or you'll be forced into crappy terms or a much higher interest rate than you should pay.

This will make you sick: Many hospitals now ask for your social security number on admission. Then they'll run a credit report behind the scenes that includes a proprietary scoring model to calculate the odds that they'll get paid.

With over 4.5 billion pieces of information getting stuffed into files each month, errors happen a lot. According to a study by the California Public Interest Research Group Education Fund, here are some pretty staggering statistics about the accuracy of credit bureau reports:

25% of reports contained errors so serious they could result in the denial of credit.

54% of credit reports contained incorrect information, or outdated and wrong accounts.

8% of files had missing credit card, loan, or mortgage reports that would have helped boost a credit score.

30% of reports still showed or reported accounts as active, where the account had been closed.

Messed up and incorrect credit files don't start as being the fault of the credit bureaus. Remember that they are only a clearing house for data. The information in your file gets to them from financial institutions you deal with where inaccuracies are downloaded directly to the credit bureaus. Garbage in, equals garbage out. Most mistakes happen when your financial institution does not properly report your address, your middle name, if you are a Sr. or Jr., or other items critical to getting your information into the right file. Or, in the case of collection items which have very little information to start with, and that may not even be yours, the challenge is to get them out of your file. Where the credit bureaus are entirely at fault is in not taking consumer requests seriously enough, for deliberately hiding their contact numbers, and for not having real human beings available to deal with issues.

How to check your credit reports

It's critical that you check your credit report once a year from all three credit bureaus. According to The Fair Credit Reporting Act, every individual is entitled to one free credit report per year from each agency. You can obtain your report from each of them individually, or the Federal Trade Commission has a unified web site which will allow you to pull all of them in one place:

By mail:	Annual Credit Report Request Service
	Box 105281
	Atlanta, GA 30348-5281
By phone:	877 322 8228
Online:	www.annualcreditreport.com

Like any other checkup, it's a good idea to review your file frequently to maintain the accuracy of the content, and to be aware of potential identity theft. After all, you cannot change what you don't know. Different lenders deal with different credit reporting agencies. Some will report your information to all three agencies while others will only share data with one or two. That's the reason each of your reports can contain a variety of different information, and the reason you'll need to see all three files. In fact, studies have shown that your credit score (comprised of the information in your files) can vary by as much as 50 points between reports.

Credit Bureaus contact information:

Equifax Information Service Center

Consumer contact number:	800 685 1111
Report order number:	800 685 1111
Fraud alert & reporting line:	800 525 6285
Web site:	www.equifax.com

Experian National Consumer Assistance Center

Consumer contact number:	888 397 3742
Report order number:	888 397 3742
Fraud alert & reporting line:	888 397 3742
Disputing report content:	866 200 6020
Web site:	www.experian.com

TransUnion Credit Information Company
Consumer contact number: 800 916 8800
Report order number: 800 888 4213
Fraud alert & reporting line: 800 680 7289
Web site: www.transunion.com

When free is very expensive

There are also other companies who claim to supply free credit reports. However, they usually require you to subscribe to a monthly monitoring service. Be informed before you click, no matter how much you have to dig around their web sites. Better yet, just don't click. If you're being charged for one of these plans, you should cancel it immediately.

Recent new regulations require that these 'con sites' promising free credit reports and must disclose they aren't the real thing. They now also need to include a prominent notice on their television ads to that effect. These firms charge huge monthly fees in order for you to get your free report. A few of these companies have made over $1 billion convincing more than 12 million people that they are getting value from them. The real and only site for your free annual reports from each of the three credit bureaus is through www.annualcreditreport.com.

Common errors in your report

Errors in your credit file come in all forms and degrees of severity. Here are some of the more common issues:

- Spouse – This information can be outdated or incorrect. While it is not part of the rating, it can easily be updated, but isn't used in lending or your credit score.

- Current address – This is generated by the last inquiry. Before the file is accessed, the credit grantor enters the basic information, which locates the correct file and also uses that information as the latest update. This information may have been entered incorrectly. It is also easy to correct.

- Paid out accounts not accurate – It is possible that a computer burp, oversight, or other error can cause a paid-down or paid-in-full account to be shown incorrectly. Any incorrect payments, or balances that are higher than the actual amount, can affect future borrowing. It causes your total debt and payments to be inaccurately high, which will matter on your credit score. In these cases, the credit bureaus will require proof that the account is paid in full and will contact the lender for verification. For these reasonably easy fixes, it's also worthwhile to contact your lender directly to re-input their information accurately.

- Inaccurately paid accounts, which still show up, may also be the result of a bankruptcy. A creditor may list the item as owing and past due, forever and ever. Dispute the item with the credit bureau using documentation from your trustee. This will prove that the item was actually included in a bankruptcy and therefore shouldn't continue to be shown separately or as an active item.

- Collections not cleared – While these will stay on your file for many years, there is a big difference between a paid and settled account, and a collection item which is still owed. These items tend to be debts that have been turned over to collection agencies which focus far more on the collection effort than in updating files. It's critical that the status and balance of these items is updated accurately.

- Negative item isn't yours – Credit bureaus also obtain information from bankruptcy registers, court records, and collection agencies. Often these files are referenced by only a debtor's name and address. Their information rarely includes birth dates or social security numbers, which leaves a lot of room for error. It's the reason incorrect information is almost always negative. Disputing that an item isn't yours in the first place is quite common and will likely get removed quickly when the credit bureau or collection agency can't prove that the item is actually yours.

- Good credit references missing – It's your right to have your credit file complete, as well as accurate. When a loan or other account is missing, it's worth requesting that the item be reported to the credit bureaus, especially for anyone with minimal credit references. It only makes sense to have as many positive references as possible, which includes accounts already paid in full over the past few years.

If you have a subprime loan, make sure it gets reported to the credit bureaus. It's the least you can expect for the massively high interest rate you are paying. Unfortunately, a lot of subprime lenders don't report your on-time payments. You can bet that they will instantly report any arrears, but not always the good news. It's immoral and wrong, and should be illegal to just report selectively, but it happens a lot. Subprime lenders are interested in retaining your business, which only happens when your credit score stays low. Your goal is the opposite, to get your credit repaired in order to 'graduate' back to receiving competitive interest rates.

Disputing errors in your report

Almost 22% of consumers who order a report,
end up filing a dispute because of an inaccuracy.
Consumer Data Industry Association

By law, the Federal Credit Reporting Act mandates credit reporting agencies to correct inaccurate or incomplete information. The most important point for you to remember is to put your disputes in writing and assure that you keep copies of everything you submit for correction.

If you've obtained your report online, the dispute form comes with your report. You'll need to print out whatever you're sending as a dispute. If your report arrived by mail, you'll need to make a photocopy of everything you're sending back, then mail the dispute by registered mail, return receipt requested. It'll be your only proof of submission and will hold the credit bureaus accountable to reply to you within 30 days as required by law. By mail, it's also helpful for you to include a copy of the credit report you've obtained, highlighting the items in dispute. In the case of identity theft, you will also have to include a copy of the police report.

If you need them again, here are the links to start your dispute:

A standard one-page credit bureau dispute form is on this book's website of www.startfightingback.com.

Equifax on line dispute link: www.equifax.com – then go to: customer service.

Experian online dispute link: www.experian.com – go to: personal – then dispute.

TransUnion online dispute link: www.transunion.com – go to: credit disputes.

In addition to being organized with all your copies, you will need to be patient and persistent in contacting (or checking) with the different reporting agencies on each of the three credit bureau files you have. For a few months, following up this dispute may become a part-time job. What you will receive sooner or later is one of the following responses from the credit bureau:

No reply: You have proof of the date you submitted the dispute. Re-send the information with a note that they are now in breach of The Fair Credit Reporting Act, that the 30-day window has expired, and they must now remove the item by law or you will seek the assistance of an attorney.

Confirmation letter indicating they have started the investigation: This is just a way to stall, to extend their 30-day window, but at least something is happening.

Rejection letter: They believe that the issue is 'frivolous or irrelevant.' If the item does not impact your actual report (such as an irrelevant previous address), it's fine. If you believe they are mistaken, you will need to re-dispute the matter with a different reasoning than previously submitted.

A letter confirming the correction: They will provide an updated copy of your file – which is the result you were looking for, where the item(s) has been corrected, deleted, or amended.

Eight million people a year file a dispute with the credit bureaus. But what you and they don't know is that, "it's extremely unlikely that anyone with the authority to resolve your dispute will actually ever see it." That's according to a recent 60 Minutes investigative report. What you may not know is that your carefully documented dispute is sent to India, the Philippines, or Chile. At that point, it's changed to a simple two digit code of 'claims not his' or 'account paid in full', with a two line summary at best. It's then electronically sent to the creditor who has to reply within 30-days. One computer just asks another computer (at your lender), to confirm that the item is legitimate.

Each credit bureau deals with thousands of disputes a day. It is only an automated computer coded request, and it's not like the company who placed the item is really that interested in getting it corrected. So be ready to re-dispute the matter when it escalates to something more serious. At times, it is also helpful if you're able to contact your lender directly to correct their files.

Mike DeWine, the Ohio Attorney General has now launched an investigation into the credit bureaus. By law, they are required to actually investigate errors. "They're not doing a reasonable investigation. They're not doing an investigation at all!" claims Mike DeWine to 60 Minutes.

If your dispute is an incorrect item in your file, you'll be forced to deal with the credit bureaus. If it's an incorrect balance, a paid item still showing, or arrears that aren't accurate, start with the company who put the item on your file. The credit bureaus broadcast it to the world, but the lender who reported it can quickly update your file and send the new and correct information to the bureaus. It may save you a year or more of disputes.

If all else fails, file a complaint with the Federal Trade Commission and the Consumer Financial Protection Bureau. If the matter is serious enough, take it to small claims court where you won't need an attorney. Even by starting proceedings you will almost always get noticed and helped. If you do go to court, the credit bureaus often settle the matter, as it is less costly to make you go away, than it is to change their procedures. Just make sure you add your lender to the lawsuit. After all, it's the lender who is reporting the incorrect information in the first place.

For the credit bureaus, none of this additional work generates any income. Their profit is made by selling reports. Giving you a free report and then spending a bunch of time fixing it, is something they are mandated to do by law, or it wouldn't happen. It may also be worth asking whether the unspoken mindset of credit bureaus is to ignore a bunch of damaging information in files, as that is what lenders like to see since it lets them charge higher interest rates...

As information goes into your file from your lenders, one of the biggest preventative steps to avoid errors is to consistently use the same name on every application to reduce the chance of confusing your credit file with someone else's. Variations such as Mike or Michael, Michael A. or Michael Andrew, make referencing more difficult, if not impossible. The more common your name, the more critical it is to consistently use your full first and middle name on all accounts and all applications – all the time.

> *Great news: The Consumer Financial Protection Bureau, an agency set up specifically to help and protect you has now taken on the responsibility of regulating credit bureaus. One of their first announced actions was to indicate they're looking into changes to the dispute resolution process!*

Credit freeze

A credit freeze allows you to block anyone from having access to your credit bureau. If creditors can't look at your credit file, they won't open an account. The credit freeze can be used as a fraud alert on your file, once you've proven an identity theft violation to the credit bureaus. It's something that is always available free of charge for a 90-day period. A credit freeze is the most powerful and effective way to prevent identity thieves from fraudulently accessing credit as they attempt to be you. Nothing else is safer, better, easier, or more effective.

The process to set up a credit freeze is easily done online with each of the three credit bureaus individually, at a cost of around $3 to $10 per bureau, depending on the state in which you live. You'll be given a very long security number that you will need if you ever wish to unblock your account. To 'thaw' your file, and allow someone to run your credit report, takes just a few minutes and requires you to enter that security number. You can thaw your account in a matter of minutes when applying for your own credit in order for the lender to access your file for a credit decision. After that, you can easily re-freeze your file.

One of the very few ways to freeze the credit of your minor children is to add them as authorized users on one of your credit cards. Then 60 to 90 days later, they'll have triggered a credit file and then you can freeze their reports, manually by mail. Great news, however, if you live in Maryland. In 2012 the state became the first to pass legislation forcing the credit bureaus to allow parents to freeze the credit files of their minor children. 49 states to go…

To freeze or thaw your credit file with:

Equifax:	Online at: www.equifax.com	
	By phone:	800 272 9281
Experian:	Online at: www.experian.com	
	By phone:	888 397 3742
TransUnion:	Online at: www.transunion.com	
	By phone:	888 909 8872

Your rights under the Fair Credit Reporting Act

The following are some basic highlights related to your credit bureau file and what lenders and the bureaus are required to do:

- Fraud alert: You have the right to request a fraud alert on your file for 90 days. With a proper identity theft report from a law enforcement agency, this can be extended for a period of up to seven years. It also assures that this alert is included with all credit reports and credit scores. Credit grantors cannot extend credit, change limits, or issue new credit cards without contacting the consumer and taking reasonable verification steps. Credit bureaus are also obligated to share fraud alerts with each other to assure consumers can protect themselves with one telephone call. Anyone with an extended fraud alert is also entitled to two free credit reports in the first year.

- Trade line blocking: The credit bureaus must block fraudulent trade reports in a file when a proper identity-theft report has been filed. This measure is designed to prevent the spread of incorrect information beyond the damage that has already been done to you.

- Records disclosure: With a proper police report you have the right to obtain copies of records, as well as information from businesses where the identity theft occurred and establishments where these accounts were opened. Businesses at that point have 30 days to supply the full documentation to you.

- Reinvestigation: Credit reporting agencies have up to 45 days to reinvestigate items when you re-dispute after the first notice that they were not willing to change or fix the item you disputed.

- Credit bureaus reasoning for your credit score: Credit reporting agencies must supply up to four reasons (key factors) which have adversely affected your score (if you purchased it).

- Mortgage lenders must supply credit scores: All mortgage lenders must supply the credit score, and information on the key reasons for it, to anyone who has applied for a mortgage with them, and at no charge to the consumer.

- Notification of negative information: Lenders who supply negative information to credit reporting agencies are required to advise you that this has been (or is being) done. This is designed to make consumers aware that their credit file has (or is about to be) adversely affected.

- Higher rates must be explained: Lenders are required to provide you with your credit score when they are charging you with anything other than their best rates or terms. This applies when terms and/or rates are "materially less favorable than the most favorable terms available to a substantial portion of consumers." In other words, this disclosure applies when the rate being charged to you is significantly higher than the average client would pay.

How long items stay on your file

Items in your credit file stay on record for various lengths of time, and can vary by state. Their general parameters are as follows:

Inquiry on your file – up to two years; however, they will only impact your credit score in the first year.

Judgments – purge at longest, seven years from date filed, whether paid or not. (5 years in New York)

Collections – both paid and unpaid stay a maximum of seven years from their date of last activity supplied. (5 years in New York)

Trade items – No actual fixed timeframe exists to remove trade items; however, credit bureaus generally leave them on your file for at least seven and up to 10 years from the date of last activity.

Credit cards – always updated as a credit card continues to stay active. Missed payments showing a past due record will drop off before seven years of the transaction.

Bankruptcy – ten years from the date of filing. A discharged chapter 13 bankruptcy remains on file seven years from the date of filing.

Debt management plans – purge after seven years or less.

Tax liens, U.S. government insured and guaranteed student loans – are dropped seven years from the date the lien is paid in full. Unpaid tax liens usually stay on file in definitely.

Banks and Banking: What to Do – What to Avoid

News story: A Wall Street analyst is now recommending the stock of one of the big banks. This one has decided to focus on profits and will stop making a big effort to keep customers satisfied, or deal with a lot of complaints.

The analyst sees this as great news since the bank will no longer spend time and money on helping customers, but focus entirely on profitability, which will make the bank's stock go up!

At the center of the banking crisis, that still hasn't healed itself for millions of Americans, were most of the six biggest banks. Fifteen years ago, they had assets equal to 17% of the U.S. economic output of goods and services, called the GDP. Today, they have assets of $9.5 trillion, which is more than 65% of the entire economy! It certainly proves the old saying that, what doesn't kill you, makes you stronger.

It's a safe bet that this saying doesn't apply to your investments over the past few years, or your income, or your standard of living since these banks led the way into one of the most devastating recessions since the depression. Yet, there hasn't been a single one of them accepting responsibility for any of their actions. Even the settlements in the billions of dollars with various government agencies were all done and paid for without admitting any wrongdoing. Nobody stepped forward and acknowledged their role in the millions of families now living a financial nightmare. Barely a year after the official end of the recession, the CEO of Barclays Banks stated that "there was a period of remorse and apology for banks. That period needs to be over." If there was ever any period of remorse, you likely missed it, too.

After literally trillions of dollars of your money to bail them out, the big banks were back in the black within two years. They were more profitable than ever, while the millions of families they threw under the bus still hadn't recovered from the devastation of their financial hopes, dreams, jobs, or credit scores. After repaying their bailouts, almost all the banks were back to being even more profitable than before, and along the way, had raised all of your fees and interest to help them recover their lost income. They were back on top, and the massive increases in fees and service charges actually put them way ahead of the game. Throughout the financial crisis, they also grew bigger – a lot bigger. With more than 450 banks closing between 2008 and 2012, the big six took over many of them, as well as various investment firms and mortgage lenders who were in even more trouble than they were.

To calm you down, the media showed a lot of Congressional hearings and a lot of discussions that took up a ton of TV talk-show time. But at the end of the day, the banks and other financial institutions got good value from their millions of dollars in campaign donations and lobbying efforts: proposed legislation either never saw the light of day, or was so incredibly watered down it was almost meaningless. You have one vote every two years, but you don't have a lobbyist working for you in Washington the rest of the time. Financial institutions, on the other hand, get a vote every hour of every day. There are more than three lobbyists for every member of Congress from the financial services industry alone. All the information on the banks lobbying efforts and financial contributions is easily accessed at: www.opensecrets.org.

History will repeat itself. Yes, there will be another massive financial crisis. Stupidity and greed will always be legal, encouraged, and a great motivator for many. Many will opt for greed at all cost, often bending or breaking the law, or at least being on the wrong side of many moral issues. The banks didn't really learn any substantial lessons. And why should they? They made staggering amounts of money in interest and fees on mortgages ranging from questionable to borderline fraudulent, that they then sold off to Wall Street who bundled them up, ran them through the blender to take pieces of this one with that one, and sold them off again.

New regulations do have some disincentives to reduce excessive risk taking, but the banks are still able to do all kinds of questionable and risky maneuvers through subsidiaries, hedge funds, or overseas investing. Nothing in the new law even prevents the government from stepping in to bail out anyone again in the future. Nor does the law stop the Federal Deposit Insurance Corporation from making loan guarantees, or the Federal Reserve from paying out bailout money again down the road.

Today, even if Bank of America, for example, were to be broken into six separate parts, each of them would still be bigger than the former investment firm Bear Stearns, whose collapse was one of the triggers to the recession and economic meltdown. To quote Erin Burnett, host of CNN's OutFront, "when does too big to fail become too big to bail out"? A good question – and the line of too big to manage was actually crossed a long time ago.

However, credit should be given to Jamie Diamond, the Chairman and CEO of JP Morgan Chase, who stated on Meet the Press: "We support too big to fail. We want the government to take down a big bank... and when it happens I believe compensation should be clawed back, the board (of directors) should be fired, the equity should be wiped out, and the bank should be dismantled and the name should be burned in disgrace." Now if only Congress would write that into law...

Overdrafts

New legislation in 2010 closed the door for banks to automatically charge you to overdraft your account. The year before, the banks had earned $37 billion in overdraft fees. Until then, a zero balance was never really zero, because they would automatically do you the favor of overdrafting your account.

You will now need to opt-in – to specifically give your bank permission to overdraw your account. Yes, banks will continue to market this service like crazy in order to protect their tens of billions of dollars in fees, but don't fall for it. All you'll be doing is agreeing to let your bank take an average overdraft fee of $36 every time – and often more than once. If you choose to avoid it, you will no longer get charged a $30 overdraft for a $3 coffee. An even worse case showed a note from a man whose $1.00 Red Box movie rental caused a $34 overdraft on his account.

Your best bet is to not sign up for overdraft protection, no matter how much the bank wants to sell you on the idea that 'it's for your protection.' Don't do it. In fact, after the rollout of the new laws, one of the big six banks actually sent a letter to their customers with a warning that your debit card "may not work the same way anymore, even if you just made a deposit, unless we hear from you." Talk about a scare tactic to get customers into the branch to sign them up for overdrafts. With a lot of heat and media attention, the bank sent out a second letter to clarify the first one. For the banks, their marketing push is certainly working. From a high of $39 billion in fees in 2009, today they're still generating around $30 billion, and charging an average of $36 to cover an average overdraft amount of $35!

If you do choose to pay for an overdraft, make sure you ask your bank if it's a flat amount (where a $1 overdraft charges you their full $30 to $40 fee), or whether it's a staggered fee. In that case, you will be charged a smaller fee for a smaller overdraft. A few banks will now waive overdraft charges for anything under $10 or so and some have lowered their charges. A much better plan is to have your own real overdraft protection. Have your bank link your checking account to your savings or other account. That way, when you do need to overdraw your account, the bank will automatically transfer the money from your other designated account. You will be covering your own overdraft at a much lower charge, instead of using the bank's money!

How one overdraft can cost $150 or more

Logic would dictate that, if you overdraw your account one day, even with three or four transactions, it's overdrawn for the day, right? Well – no. According to a Federal Reserve survey, and millions of really upset people, banks can and often do clear your charges from largest to smallest. With something called overdraft software maximization banks can re-order what they post through your account. It's not done at the time you do the transaction in chronological order, but shuffled around at the end of the day to the benefit of the bank. Why? Because it will generate two or three overdraft or NSF charges, instead of just one.

Suppose you lost track of your balance and had signed up for overdraft protection. Let's say your balance was $100. On one day you used your debit card for a $40 cash withdrawal, a $20 grocery store charge, and $15 for lunch. Plus, that night, your rent payment also came out of your account for $400. Since there are now four debits totaling $475, you'll be overdrawn and should pay an overdraft fee. But it's not that simple with many banks who re-order those charges.

You had a $100 balance and the $40, $20, and $15 should have cleared and left a balance of $25 before the rent of $400 overdrafted you. Yet, if your bank just holds these debits until that night, their computer can shuffle them to get more than one overdraft! If they put through the rent of $400 first, you're already in the hole. THEN they'll put through the other three charges. The rent puts you into overdraft charge number one. Then they will process the other three charges and collect four overdraft fees instead of one! Just by processing these in a different order, they've maximized their fees and have thrown you under the bus.

> *One small example of processing charges from highest to lowest involved a class action lawsuit against Wells Fargo in California. The judge, who ordered Wells Fargo to re-pay $203 million in overdraft fees, wrote that the policy was to "squeeze as much as possible" out of customers who were overdrawing their accounts. The bank's online statement showed items in chronological order, but that was not how their software was clearing the items. The judge also did not accept the bank's argument that their customers wanted this, and actually benefited from what they were doing. Needless to say, Wells Fargo disagreed with the ruling and is appealing the decision.*

Your bank accounts

> *What's the balance in your checking account? In February 2013, the finance minister of Zimbabwe admitted that the country's public accounts had a balance of only $217.*

The only reason to deal with a bank is to have a place to park some of your money. Just like you don't take your vehicle to a grocery store for service, don't go to a bank to do any kind of investing. The purpose of these financial institutions is for you to have your basic checking and savings accounts. That's assuming you deal with one that has low or no fee accounts, you plan to have your pay deposited, and you want to utilize their online services.

Unfortunately, there's a direct correlation to the size of the bank and the lack of service you'll get. Almost every study and satisfaction survey shows that the larger the financial institution, the worse their customer service. For them, it's a numbers game, and with tens of millions of customers, losing your business isn't something they'd notice or care about.

> *I strongly believe in a paraphrased saying that you can easily judge a business by how they treat those who can do nothing for them – in other words, how you get treated when you need help, and not when a business will make a profit from you.*
>
> *My father recently died and I became executor of his estate. After I had all the legal documents, I went to the bank branch where he had dealt for many decades. All I wanted to do was turn in his credit and ATM card to have them closed, and to have his accounts blocked. It started off badly and got worse. The receptionist asked me three times if I had an appointment. No sorry, I didn't, and I was only in town for the funeral, and to handle these basic starter issues on the estate. "Nobody has time unfortunately – we do have clients with appointments." What I wanted to say was that my dad didn't die with an appointment, but I managed to simply ask to speak to a manager. Surely someone in this huge branch would have five minutes for me.*
>
> *An assistant manager did come out to also ask if I had an appointment. At that point, my perception was that this question was just code for 'please just go away.' She did volunteer other branches that may be able to help me.*

What? I can't get into the branch that had more than $1 million of his deposits? Did she really believe I'd have more success at a branch that hadn't made some significant income from my dad over all these years?

After about half an hour I did get to meet with an account manager. When she took me into that wing, there were about 14 offices in that area. Three had their lights out, making me figure that those staff had the day off. But 11 offices did not have a single customer in any office! A half hour at reception fighting to get in, being re-educated that I really should have an appointment, and in the 10 minutes I was in the office wing there wasn't a single customer – anywhere!

After that, my only option was to start communicating through the estate attorney… at $375 an hour… even after one of their Vice Presidents contacted me to apologize that the branch had certainly dropped the ball. By that time, my only drive was to get everything transferred out as soon as possible.

As banks lost a large part of their revenues from overdraft fees, they immediately started looking elsewhere to reach into your wallet. One of the first and easiest targets was to implement fees for basic checking accounts. That now holds true for over fifty percent of all accounts. How much their fees are depends on the bank and the type of account you hold. When banks first started a serious effort to implement these fees, some banks tested the amount you'd be willing to pay before closing your account and going elsewhere. Some took tens of thousands of accounts, or did it by region, and tested four, five, or six dollar charges. When there wasn't much pushback at different price points, they knew they were well on the way to maximizing their profits.

When you open a new account, you may not realize that the bank will run a credit report on you. Depending on your credit score, banks will put a hold on any check deposited for a certain number of days. Whether you've had your account for a long time, or just opened it, you will need to know specifically when their system will decide to hold a check. They may hold a percentage of a larger check, such as 25% of any deposit over $2,000, or may hold every deposit for a certain number of days. If you don't ask, and don't know, you may be spending a bunch of the money on NSF fees or overdraft charges. If you've had your account for some time, you can also have the bank adjust your hold amounts. It will require them to do another credit check and to update their computers, but you have to ask.

My bank has a new service where they will text you your balance. It's cool, I just don't think they should add "lol" at the end. FB post

Banks do have to disclose any new fees they intend to roll out, and the business is still competitive. You may also have your monthly charge waived if your average balance is above a certain amount, so shop around. Make sure that one of the places you contact is your local credit union. Almost all of them will still have some kind of free checking account.

What you didn't know can cost you

Included in the documents you sign for a loan, HELOC, or overdraft protection, there is almost always a clause called Right of Offset. In English, it means that your financial institution can take any money you have with them, and apply it towards your debt if you are in arrears. And, they can do this without notice to you. If you're behind on your payments, they can empty your checking account or any other money you have on deposit and move it towards your loan, HELOC, or any other borrowing.

Credit cards, however, are exempt from this law. While you certainly never plan to get behind, it's critical to never have any substantial amounts of money at the same place that also holds your loan or HELOC – just in case something does happen.

> *Susan is 74 years old and retired. Two years ago she co-signed a $5,000 loan for her granddaughter. When her granddaughter lost her job, she was not able to continue making the $260 payments on the loan. Unfortunately, it was something she didn't tell her grandmother. When the loan went two months in arrears, the bank took the entire balance of $1,460 out of her checking account to pay towards the loan balance. Living only on social security, it devastated Susan's finances for over a year. If that wasn't enough, within a few days, the bank was calling to collect what was now a $31 overdraft charge.*

If you have a problem

A study from Pew Safe Foundation found that the median length of a fee and account disclosure for a simple checking account is 69 pages. Some are upwards of 150 or more, and two-thirds of accounts include a clause taking away your right to outside help in resolving complaints and problems.

In that tiny print, even attorneys would have a hard time understanding the clause which states that disputes with the bank have to be dealt with through arbitration and not the courts. While you cannot even take them to small claims court, the disclosure doesn't point out that 99.5% of the time arbitrators rule in favor of the bank. To add insult to injury, the Pew report also found that most disclosure forms state that even if banks lose in arbitration, you'll have to pay their costs.

The odds of winning an arbitration hearing against a bank are 1 in 200. And if you're that one 'winner', you will likely pay way more in costs than the arbitration will award you. Toss a coin. Heads, the bank wins – tails, you lose.

The complex section explaining arbitration really ought to read, "… you have no chance of ever fighting us on anything in the world. Deal with it, as there is zero chance you will ever get compensated for anything, at any time, no matter how badly we messed up." What's puzzling is why you would still deal with the big banks.

As a result, your only recourse is to file a complaint with the regulatory agencies. If you do, let your financial institution know that you've already filed a complaint. Knowing that you know your rights and you will not go away until you have your issue resolved, can often get you the help and attention you should have received in the first place.

If your financial institution is regulated by your state, it will be with the state's banking regulators. You can find the contact information at 800-FED-INFO (333-4636). If it's federally regulated, contact the Federal Reserve at 888-851-1920. Both are online at: www.usa.gov – then go to: topics – consumer protections.

The Consumer Financial Protection Bureau which now has responsibility for a range of bank complaints can be reached at: 855-411-2372 or online at: www.consumerfinance.gov.

Complaints filed against banks with the CFPB
receive a response within 15-days 95% of the time.
Which banks get the largest percentage of complaints filed?
In a recent 14-month period it was:
Bank of America (32%) and Wells Fargo (19%).

If your complaint involves a credit union, contact the National Credit Union Administration Office of Consumer Protection at 800-755-1030, or online at: www.mycreditunion.gov.

If you can't bank on the big banks

100 million Americans belong to a credit union.
Hopefully you're already one of them.

On the opposite scale of the too-big-to-fail banks are vast numbers of local and regional banks and credit unions. None of them needed or received bailout money, and these are the places where you should have your accounts. They actually know their customers and members, and they genuinely care. Credit unions, and most local and regional banks, were started on your main street, and not on Wall Street. To paraphrase USA Today: Credit unions have one real asset they own which nobody can match, and that's their relationship with their customers.

It's your choice. You can deal with a call center that may be located in India, or an outsourced firm who likely gets paid on call volumes. Or you can deal with a local community bank or credit union, where even the president and board of directors probably all live within 50 miles of you. Make your local credit union one of your stops when shopping for your financial needs. They're not-for-profit financial cooperatives whose sole purpose is to meet the needs of their members. With over 7,000 credit unions in all 50 states, almost a third of the population deals with them and is familiar with their good service, friendly approach, and extensive community involvement.

Credit union rates and products are always competitive
with other financial institutions, and often better. To find

out if that's true, check the Credit Union National Association which has a daily update of rates and fees. It compares the banks' averages with credit unions on everything from credit cards to savings, HELOCs to mortgages at: www.creditunion.coop.

Where credit unions excel, head and shoulders above others, is in their member service. Yes, you will be a member-owner and not just a customer. It might not sound like much, but you will quickly notice the difference. Each credit union can have different membership requirements. These are generally based on common employee groups such as teachers or fire fighters, associations, school or alumni groups, or even entire residential communities. Plus, at the end of the year you will actually receive a dividend (rebate) based on your connection with a credit union. When was the last time your bank actually paid you?

You can search for a credit union in your area through the web site called 'A Smarter Choice' which allows you to search by city or zip code. The results will link you directly to that credit union and give you some of the criteria for membership at: www.asmarterchoice.org

If, or hopefully when, you're ready to switch financial institutions, it will take a one-time effort and a few hours of your time. Start by finding a credit union or regional bank and setting up your new account. That will be the majority of your leg work in getting started. After that, almost all have switch-kits that will help you with transferring your direct deposits and other automatic debits coming from your account. It's worth the one-time effort, and you'll get paid back more from the money you save and the service you'll receive.

Your Credit Score: A Wrong Number Can Cost You a Lot

Myths, lies, misunderstandings, frightening stories, and ads from for-profit companies trying to sell you, have created an entire country of people who generally know how important their credit score is, but not much more. And what most people think they know just isn't true.

More and more of you live in a world that knows you by one number or another, instead of your name. From your PIN to your social security and employee number, many of these are unavoidable. But there's one number that tells the world a lot more about you than any other, and not always accurately; it's arguably the most important number in your life: your credit score.

That magical number between 300 and 850 is calculated off a super-secret formula that nobody really understands, but controls more parts of your life than you realize – in way more areas of your life than it should. It really is the one number you may not want to live without.

Nothing about your credit score is black and white. The various parts of your score that will move up or down depend entirely on your handling of credit. Anything you did (or didn't do) will raise or drop your score. But how long anything negative will take to correct, depends on a number of factors that are unique to you and your credit report. In other words, there isn't a sure-fire answer that states, if you do this or that, your score will move up by 27 points on February 12th next year. The good news is that the basics of what impacts your score aren't difficult to understand, so it is possible to have total control over what you want your score to be. The actions you take today won't always move your score in the next month or two, but eventually, the score *will* change.

Who cares?

If the average American raises their credit score by only 30 points,
it would save over $20 billion a year in interest!
Consumer Federation of America Study

If you had two friends, who wanted to borrow money from you, and you knew with statistical certainty that one would pay you back and the other would not, would you want that information to make a decision? Of course! That's the reason for your credit score, which all lenders use as one of their main sources in evaluating your credit worthiness. It's the key tool used to make billions of credit decisions each year, as well as setting the interest rates you'll be charged for almost any borrowing. It works, it's consistent, it's easy to apply, and it takes away any discrimination of race, gender, etc. It's also fast and accurate (assuming your credit file is accurate, and that's a big assumption…)

Unfortunately, it's also massively overused and an easy and lazy way to make decisions that shouldn't be based solely on some score. Who cares? You may care, if you knew the vast areas of your life where your credit score is used:

Any type of borrowing	All low rate vehicle loans
Opening a bank account	ATM holds on deposits
ATM withdrawal limits	Bonding applications
Pay as you go at gas stations	Credit card solicitations
Every credit card interest rate	Landlords
Credit card limits	Job applications
Almost all insurance rates	PMI (mortgage insurance)
Rent-a-Car agencies	Hospitals and medical field

Military security clearances	Some dating websites
Employment hiring decisions	Promotions or layoff
Getting an insurance or broker's license in some states	

While it may make sense to base an actual credit decisions on your credit score, does it make sense for a landlord to use it? Does it make sense in the medical field? More and more hospitals are adopting a new software program to determine your ability and your willingness to pay. They'll include your credit score in their calculations, but also go way further to include the payment history on any previous medical bills, available limits on credit cards, as well as balances in your 401(k) plans. In the military over 20% of security clearance applications are rejected based on credit scores. In the Navy, according to the Department of Defense, upwards of 80% of security clearance revocations are the result of low credit scores. And you wonder why a dating website would care? Well, at least one requires you to have a credit score over 760 before you can join. If you prefer to rent a car with a debit card, some companies like Dollar will pull your credit report if you're not using a credit card for deposit.

Is it right or fair that your next promotion or even job application may be partially based on your credit score? The majority of prison sentences aren't as long as the punishment to your score! Plus, you may now be caught in a vicious cycle and a catch-22 – you need the income to get current on bills but have a difficult time getting hired when large numbers of employers pull your credit score and use it as a factor in making their hiring decision.

In the next few years things will get worse and not better. Marginal lenders have taken some steps to using information from social networks to score your credit worthiness. One company, Neo, already uses software to confirm jobs by looking at LinkedIn with your permission. An online lender, ZestFinance, and Kreditech, a German start-up, already looks at your Facebook data. A New York based on-line bank now monitors your Facebook messages and can cut your credit card rates if you're talking them up with your friends. If some of those methods sound very wrong, are massively overused in making oversimplified decisions, or are just stupid, you're correct.

620 versus 720

A 100 point rise in your credit score will save you $118,500 over the next 30-years, and almost $4,000 a year!

You may know the impact a 100 point change in your credit score can have, but you probably haven't thought about the consequences over your lifetime. With some very conservative assumptions, what exactly is the financial impact between a 620 and a 720 score? These examples use the difference in interest costs over 30-years. If you're 40 or younger, this could be you, without the tools and help to move your score:

• $8,036 on your credit cards. In the new borrowing reality, your 620 score will get you a rate of 19.8%, but only if you're lucky, according to CardHub. That's significantly higher than the 12.9% a 720 score will get you. That's based on an average balance of $14,000, assuming minimum payments are being made, and you never charge anything ever again.

• $20,856 for your vehicle loans. Assuming you'll finance a vehicle every seven years for $25,000, a pretty conservative assumption, the difference in interest rates is even more staggering. With a 620 score, you'll likely end up paying subprime rates. If you can manage to avoid those, you'll still end up with four vehicle loans in your lifetime at a rate of at least 10%. Compare this to 3% or better for a 720 score at almost any credit union.

- $57,600 on your mortgage loan. With a $200,000 loan, even assuming you'll never refinance, the 100 point difference in your score translates to a rate difference of 1.37%, as quoted by myfico.

- $7,509 on an average $35,000 HELOC with a standard 10-year draw of interest only and then a 10-year repayment, according to myfico.

- $16,605 on your insurances. With the national average auto insurance of $1,577, according to Carinsure, a 100 point rise in your credit score will reduce your premiums by at least 25%, or $394 annually. On the average $638 home insurance policy, quoted by homeinsure.com, the savings would translate to $160 annually. Both assume an accident-free record for five years and a claims-free home owner policy.

- $7,920 with private student loans. Federal loans don't use credit scores; however, private loans do – and in a big way. Based on quotes from Sallie Mae, a $20,000 fixed rate student loan will cost you or save you 6.1%, depending on your score.

Do you know what goes into your credit score?

If you spend the time reading this chapter and understanding the insights, tricks, traps, and factors of your credit score, you'll be better informed than 90% of the population. Without it, you can't change or fix what you don't know. The following list consists of the most commonly asked questions used in calculating your score. The answers are at the end of the chapter, but begin by testing your own knowledge.

Is this item part of your credit score calculation?

Applying for any type of credit	y	n
Applying for credit but getting declined	y	n
Applying for overdraft protection	y	n
Arrears by someone you co-signed for	y	n
Authorized user on someone's credit card	y	n
Bad credit account beyond Statute of Limitation	y	n
Bankruptcy	y	n
Being a victim of identity theft	y	n
Borrowing from your 401(k)	y	n
Cell phone contract	y	n
Change in income (up or down) or job title	y	n
Checking your own credit report	y	n
Closing a credit card	y	n
Collection agency pulling your credit file	y	n
Corrections to personal information on credit bureau	y	n
Co-signing anything for anyone	y	n
Credit card issuers updating their files	y	n
Credit card transfers to lower rate cards	y	n
Credit counseling	y	n
Credit monitoring	y	n
Credit utilization (percentage you owe vs. your limits)	y	n
Debit card usage	y	n
Debt settlement (on your own or through a company)	y	n
Defaulting on a pawnshop loan	y	n
Defaulting on a payday loan	y	n
Disputing an item in your credit file	y	n
Don't pay for six months or a year finance plan	y	n
Early termination of contract by paying penalty fee	y	n
Employment or employment history	y	n
Filing for bankruptcy	y	n
Foreclosure or short sale	y	n

Fraud alert on your credit bureaus y n
Freezing your credit report y n
Getting a judgment against you y n
Getting divorced or separated y n
Getting sued y n
Going past due on any monthly payments y n
Having a mortgage-free home y n
Having or using an overdraft y n
Having your name on any debts after divorce y n
How much you pay a month on your credit card y n
Identity theft protection coverage y n
Inactive credit card y n
Increasing your credit card balance(s) y n
Increasing your credit card limit(s) y n
Interest rate on an account y n
Landlord pulling your credit report y n
Layaway plans y n
Length of time you've had your credit file y n
Marital status or getting married y n
Partner getting a new loan in his or her name only y n
Pawnshop or title loans y n
Payday lender loans y n
Paying off or paying down a loan or credit card y n
Pre-paid cards y n
Refinancing a loan y n
Rental agreements y n
Secured credit car y n
Shopping around for one loan in a month y n
Store (retailer) credit card application y n
Tax lien y n
Type of credit accounts you have y n
Where you live y n
Your total wealth or assets y n

The good, the bad and the ugly scores

If you know the critical (if not stupid and questionable) reasons your credit score gets used by seemingly everybody on the planet, you need to know some broad common score levels. When the economy is good, lenders will lower their threshold score to accept more business. Conversely, when the economy is hurting, they'll move up their minimum score requirement to tighten up their lending, since a higher score means fewer people will qualify. However, based on your real FICO score, discussed in the next section, the following are some broad and generalized levels:

760 or higher. That's your best score and you're close enough to perfect. In credit jargon, you're golden, and lenders will offer you their best rates and terms.

720 or higher. Your credit score is just fine and you'll get the best credit card and vehicle loan rates more than 90% of the time. A few more points won't matter until, and unless, you can reach the 760 level.

700 or higher. You'll get almost every credit card and have reached the magic point of really good mortgage or refinance rates (until you get to 760).

660 or higher. For vehicle loans, you'll need to shop around as you may be told you need to pay subprime rates. Credit card issuers may approve you. Also, you're within three-quarters of a percent of the best mortgage and refinance rates.

620 or lower. Unfortunately, your score will necessitate subprime rates for almost all borrowing. Right now, there are tens of millions of Americans at or below this score.

What's the average for your fellow Americans? FICO recently stopped publishing them. For years, however, the average had been 692 and is likely still around that number. FICO did publish statistics that 46% of Americans have a score below 700 and almost 25% are below 600. The website Credit Karma reports a U.S. average on their scoring of 664.

> *The Federal government also has a credit score which is set by rating agencies. When it was downgraded, that impact created an extra $2 billion per year in interest costs on federal borrowing. In Greece, the downgrade to their debt rating caused interest rates on government borrowing to skyrocket to over 15%.*

Your real score

> *Your credit score is only based on your credit status on the particular day your score is calculated.*

In the words of financial writer Greg Karp, there's your FICO score versus your FAKO scores. While you have vast numbers of different scores which are discussed in the next section, the real one is called your FICO score. It's the original scoring model developed by Fair Isaac Company, hence the acronym FICO. It's used by more than 90% of companies when you apply for credit in their establishments. If you're looking for a range of your score, other models will do, and they're often free of charge. If you want to know exactly what your credit card issuer, bank, or mortgage lender sees, it needs to be the same scoring model that they use, which is your FICO score.

There are only two places where you can purchase your actual lender-used FICO score. The first is through the company itself at www.myfico.com. An alternate place is through Equifax, which is one of the three credit bureaus and the only one licensed by FICO to sell their scores to the public at www.equifax.com. On their site, however, the main sales focus will be for their Equifax Credit Score. It's cheaper, but it's not your FICO score. On the Equifax site, you will need to assure that you go to the bottom of the 'products' page and click on the real FICO score purchase.

Obtaining your FICO score isn't free. Yes, you're entitled to your free credit reports each year, but you'll have to pay to get your score. That isn't necessary more than once a year; besides, your score can literally change daily to some degree. If you're about to obtain some type of credit, it may be worth the time and investment to purchase your score. If you know it from a year or so ago, and nothing much has changed in your financial life, you may not need to spend the money again. Your free annual credit report will show any changes, and those will impact your score. Then you can decide if purchasing your updated score is warranted.

Tip notes come with your credit score in regards to what factors are holding it down. They're totally generic and so generalized as to be almost useless. You'll need your full credit report, not just your score. Then apply the tips and insights from this chapter to the items in your report.

Getting access to your real credit score is incredibly valuable. It's the same reason you go to the doctor for a checkup. But you need to be mindful that your credit score is a reflection of what has already happened. If that's negative, by the time you find out it's too late. However, if you understand the basics of this chapter, you will have incredible knowledge in preventing a drop in your score. You will also have the insights and tools to raise it. That's pro-active, and something which is totally within your control and power. It's kind of like the difference between getting the score of a baseball game the next day or being in the game.

You actually have over 100 credit scores

*"When consumers buy a credit score, they should be
aware that a lender may be using a very different
score in making a credit decision."*
Richard Cordray, CFPB Director

There are literally thousands of credit scoring formulas. Each of them is custom made for a specific company, based on their own needs and priorities. Their formula starts with one of your credit bureau reports and emphasises or discounts certain factors, and then adds that company's internal information. Most companies use these purely for internal use; others develop scores to sell them to you without having to get permission from Fair Issac (and having to pay their licensing fees).

Some sites require you to purchase a subscription or a credit monitoring service and they'll throw in a 'free' credit score. You can also get some of your credit scores for free with no strings attached. Sites want to draw you in to be able to sell you stuff, and they know that getting your credit score is very attractive. Unfortunately, these are not your FICO scores. Some are close, some are pretty accurate, but many are not. While free may sound great, they can also cause more confusion than insights.

Marketed under a variety of names, the rest of the scores cause confusion, have very different scales, and can be difficult to compare to the real thing. In fact, they can often lead you to a false sense of security by making you think your score is sufficient for the best rates, only to find out that it's not. It isn't hard to find many postings on message boards of people who have paid a fair amount of money for their score monitoring, only to be turned down for credit, because the lender used their real FICO score. As a result, they were out the money and back to square one.

One credit card had the credit score included with each monthly statement. When the card issuer was sold to one of the giants, the practice quickly stopped. Makes you wonder if the last thing they wanted was a bunch of credit-smart customers…

Any free credit score is useful for observing a trend. If you consistently use the same one, you'll have a great idea if you're making progress or falling back over time. What doesn't work is comparing one to another, and to your real FICO score. That will only create confusion and frustration. If you purchase your FICO score, pull one of the free ones on the same day or in the same week. Then you'll have the comparisons side by side. From then on, the free one will let you see if you're making progress. Keep in mind that free comes with a catch: you're giving these sites personal information that they'll use for targeted advertising. You don't have to purchase anything, but you will get hit with a lot of ads.

> www.creditcarma.com … will supply you with a score estimator based only on your TransUnion file.

> www.credit.com … allows access to a score estimator once per month and based on a letter grade score from your Experian file.

> www.quizzle.com … will let you see a score estimate twice a year, also based on your Experian credit file

> www.creditsesame.com … you'll get a score you can access monthly, based on your Experian file.

You also have something called a VantageScore. It was developed by all three credit bureaus, and all of them market this score which ranges from 501–990. It's their alternative to FICO, but it hasn't gained much traction or recognition with lenders.

The fee-based membership site True Credit also uses the VantageScore from each of the three bureaus.

Many credit card issuers also use a number of internal scores that you'll never hear about. A Revenue Score calculates how much money they're making from you. Their Response Score measures how likely you are to respond to new card offers or teaser rates.

Banks also use customized scores which can include a Bank Behavior Score. It's software to score you on factors ranging from your deposits, withdrawal habits, and balances. It also monitors whether your payroll deposits have stopped, as an early warning that you're potentially unemployed. Credit card companies use it to target offers to you, but also as a warning signal that there may be trouble. If you've been using your card at Saks and now the charges are from discount retailers, they can see it as advance signs of financial trouble.

Companies pay a lot of money for quality information. Credit reporting agencies keep looking for new ways to utilize all the information they have about you in order to write a new report they can sell to someone – anyone. You'll never see them, but these scoring reports include:

Bankruptcy risk scores – pro-active tools that score the mathematical odds of you going bankrupt in the future, in order to warn lenders to cut down available credit.

Pre-scores – used for advertisement campaigns and pre-approvals.

Predictive analytics models – used to figure out if you'll become a future problem client or a great marketing potential.

Revenue Score – used mainly by credit card companies and home equity lenders to find the most profitable customers.

Attrition Score – used by card issuers who will increase their bonus offers if the score shows them that you're likely dealing with a competitor card.

Collection Score – bought by collection agencies to score or rank accounts to maximize collection results (by up to 20%).

If that list doesn't sound invasive enough, Equifax also sells your employment and income information to collection agencies. One of its subsidiaries actually has that information on almost a third of all Americans. "It's the biggest privacy breach in our time" stated Robert Mather of Pre-Employ.com, in a quote to NBC.

Debt free AND a great credit score

You don't have to love debt, or be in debt, in order to have a great credit score. In fact, anyone with a credit score over 760 or so, has significantly less debt than someone with a 600 to 700 score. A credit score doesn't measure how broke you are. It is purely a measurement of how responsible you are with your available credit – whether you pay it in full every month, or over time. Your score can be just as high with limited credit over a long period of time, where you never carry a balance, or pay interest at all.

The two critical factors to getting and keeping a high credit score are: 1) never go past due on any account, and 2) get or keep your credit card balances to less than 30% of the credit limit.

In an ideal world, the best credit score would be zero. It's someone who is debt free, has nothing borrowed or financed, and doesn't have any credit cards. That would be common sense, but that's anything but common in the world of finance and credit. A zero, or non-existent credit score, simply indicates that you've either never had credit, or haven't had any credit for the past seven years. But is a zero credit score the ultimate goal, or even the wisest choice? Not necessarily, and also, not likely.

Can you get by without a credit score? Absolutely. A non-existent credit score simply means that you don't borrow money, and isn't that the position you'd like to be in? You can still get your vehicle insured, even if there may be a premium. You can still get and use a debit card. You can also be approved for a mortgage loan. It'll take a little shopping around, but just requires a lender who simply wants to base the decision on your score. It takes something called manual underwriting and likely needs you to have a standard 20% down payment, a solid job history, proof of income, and other documentation.

However, the great news is that you don't need to choose an all-or-nothing proposition. You can have a great credit score and not be in debt or have any monthly payments. With no collections or credit problems in the past seven years (when it drops off your file), one or two credit cards with decent limits, and a balance below 20% of your limit (even better below 10%), will give you a score around 800.

> *Want proof? On the next page is my credit report and score summary. With only two credit cards, my score never really changes much. If my statement balance one month goes above 30% of the limit, it'll drop for one month until the next statement. One current $1,100 limit card was lowered from $8,000 or so a few years ago. At that time, seemingly everyone else had their limits dropped too. Cutting it by 500% on an 800 score customer made no sense, but it simply meant that this card will really never get used again... their loss... but I do want and need its long track record and history.*

CREDIT REPORT *as of 03/01/2013*

Open Accounts	Total#	Balance	Available ⁇	Credit Limit ⁇	Debt to Credit	Monthly Payment Amount ⁇	Accounts with a Balance
Mortgage	0	$0	N/A	N/A	N/A	$0	0
Installment	0	$0	N/A	N/A	N/A	$0	0
Revolving	2	$522	$7,878	$8,400	6%	$22	2
Other	0	$0	N/A	N/A	N/A	$0	0
Total	2	$522	$7,878	$8,400	6%	$22	2

Account Age
Usually, it is a good idea to keep your oldest credit account open, as a high average account age generally demonstrates stability to lenders. Also, especially if you have been managing credit for a short time, opening many new accounts will lower your average account age and may have a negative impact.

Length of Credit History: 27 Years, 7 Months
Average Account Age: 11 Years, 8 Months

Oldest Account:
XXXXXXXXXXXXXXXXXX (Opened 08/01/1985)

Most Recent Account:
XXXXXXXXXXXXXXX (Opened 07/13/2009)

Potentially Negative Information
Late payments, collections and public records can have a negative impact on your credit standing.

Public Records - 0

Negative Accounts - 0

Collections - 0

Inquiries - Requests for your Credit History
Numerous inquires on your credit file for new credit may cause you to appear risky to lenders, so it is usually better to only seek new credit when you need it.

Inquiries in the Last 2 Years - 0
Most Recent Inquiry - N/A

The five factors that create your score

Your credit score doesn't just happen to you –
it is entirely within your power to control.

Your credit score comes from the information out of your credit bureau file. Five different factors make up your score, which will range between 300 and 850. All of these factors have a different value, and some are vastly more important than others. Since you can't change what you don't know, you first have to understand what goes into calculating your credit score:

35% (298 points out of 850) – your payment history of all accounts

30% (255 points out of 850) – the amounts you owe

15% (127 points out of 850) – the length of time of your credit history

10% (85 points out of 850) – the quantity of new credit applications

10% (85 points out of 850) – the types of credit accounts you have

The importance of these items actually makes a lot of common sense. You don't have to agree with them, but it's critical that you understand them.

Suppose you had a friend that wanted to borrow some money from you. Wouldn't one of the first things on your mind be whether he has or hasn't been very good at paying you back in the past? Isn't there a difference between stalling you once in the past versus almost always taking an extra month or so to pay you back? That's what makes up the payment history of your score.

If a friend already owes money to you, and everybody else on the planet, wouldn't you be a little more reluctant to lend him another $200? That's the 'total amounts owed' in your score. If you've known him for 20 minutes or 20-years, wouldn't that make a difference in your decision? Well, that's the 'length of time' part of your formal credit score. Finally, if he's asking just you, or also every other friend to lend him money, isn't that something you'd want to know, and wouldn't that raise some red flags? In your credit score, that's the 'quantity of accounts' being applied for.

Your payment history (35%)

Past behavior is used to predict future behavior. You may disagree, but it's valid, and it's the largest factor in your score.

This category calculation includes all of your past payment history which stays on file for five to seven years. Any arrears are a sure-fire way to reduce your score very quickly, as will any judgment or collection. If your score is high already, even one-time arrears can drop your score by 100 points. Should your score be in the mid 600's, the impact will be much less. For a high score, it would be very rare to get past due, which is the reason for the large drop. In the mid 600's, the score is there because of past arrears already, so the impact won't nearly be as much. In other words, a high score is way more about avoiding stupid mistakes than doing anything positive.

There is a difference, however, between a missed payment three years ago and a one-month late vehicle payment this year. While the history will reflect the arrears for years, the importance in your score diminishes over time and has a very limited impact after three years. The older the bad payment records, the less they matter.

What makes it even less important is having new accounts that are currently being paid on time every month. New, and paid-as-agreed accounts, have a larger weighting on your score than older and not so good accounts. Your score also takes into account whether the arrears were on a large installment loan such as your mortgage or vehicle loan, rather than a smaller credit card balance.

The amounts you owe (30%)

The less you owe, the more your score will grow.

While income doesn't have anything to do with your credit score, what you owe is a huge factor. Even more critical is that the scoring formula compares your credit limits, or what you originally borrowed, to the amounts you owe today. A vehicle loan starts off at 100% borrowed and owing. That just makes sense if you haven't even started your payments. It's also something you have no control over. However, a year down the road, your high credit (the amount you started with) versus what you owe will be very different. Fixed payment loans are not the primary factor in your total debt calculation in any event.

The impact or weighting on your score is heavily tilted towards revolving credit which has a balance and credit limit, such as a HELOC or credit card. Comparing your limit versus your balance is called credit utilization and it's the single biggest factor controlling your credit score next to making on-time payments. Credit utilization calculates your balance divided by your limit to get the percentage of credit you've used.

For example, if your credit card has a $5,000 limit and your balance is $2,000, dividing the $2,000 into $5,000 is a 40% utilization. If your balances are over 50% of your limits, your score will plummet. If you're below 10% you're close to maximizing your credit score from this category. This calculation looks at each revolving account one at a time and also totals all of them together. Since it's likely that you have one line of credit at most, the critical parts of your credit utilization are your credit cards. Their impact on your score is so significant that they're detailed in the next section.

The length of your credit history (15%)

Lenders love to see a very long history of credit. The longer your track record, the higher this portion of your score. Generally three years or less is considered short, while five years or longer will greatly help your score. Unfortunately, there's nothing you can do to speed up the calendar. This can be a challenge for anyone younger who has only recently established some kind of credit. A shorter history is not a big problem as long as you've been making your payments on time with the limited credit you do have.

The length of time you've had your accounts very much matters for this part of your score. If you have two credit cards active for five years, that's a long-term track record. If you've recently applied for two new ones, their history is less than a month. The average length of accounts now shrinks with these new cards. In this example, you'd have two new cards for a month and two for five years each. That now brings your average length of accounts to two and a half years. Before those two new cards, your average was five. If you need to open a new account and currently have a pretty good score, then go ahead. It'll be a short-term reduction to your credit score that will actually turn to your benefit over time.

The quantity of new credit applications (10%)

The more you apply for credit, the more your score will drop. The scoring model doesn't know if you're comparison shopping or trying to get credit from a number of places. Are you on track to increase your total debt with these applications? All your score knows is that there's going to be trouble if you are to be approved for all this additional credit and potential future debt. Multiple inquiries within a two or three month period can drop your score 15 to 30 points or more.

The system does have a built-in safeguard to allow you to shop around. If you're looking for a vehicle, as an example, all lender-coded vehicle loan inquiries into your credit report will only count as one inquiry no matter how many places you shop. Besides, common sense in your credit score says you're not buying four vehicles.

The exceptions to this 30-day window are credit cards. Every different issuer counts. A recent posting on a credit help site was from someone with an 825 score who saw it drop by over 70 points when he applied for a number of cards inside a few months. The good news is that inquiries only count in the new applications scoring for one year. After that your score knows that it has become an active credit account or didn't get opened in the first place.

The types of credit you have (10%)

This final category scores the mix of credit you're using. Are you relying only on credit cards, or is there a combination of a personal loan, cards, and maybe a vehicle payment? While it's a minor factor in your score, it may not be a good idea to have open credit accounts that you don't need or use. If they don't impact your credit utilization ratio, and if you have an annual fee to pay, you may want to consider closing a few of your more recently acquired credit cards.

As the credit report and score in the previous section shows, only two credit cards and no other borrowing still gets you close to the perfect score. That makes it reasonable to not spend a lot of time and thought on what your mix of credit is. And it's certainly never a reason to open another account or now take on a vehicle loan to think you'll improve your credit mix. Do stay away from store or retail cards. With little credit and a good score, the scoring model will wonder why you would voluntarily sign up for a super high interest rate card when you certainly had other options.

Increasing your score: It's in the cards

*Your credit card can charge you up
to 255 points on your score!*

Since the average adult has almost four credit cards and owes over $14,000 on them, how you manage them is one of the most important factors impacting your credit score. Of course, nothing is more important than making at least the minimum payment on time every month, without fail.

The critical factor is the total you owe compared to your credit limits. This so-called credit utilization is entirely within your control and can decrease your credit score significantly, and very quickly. Should your credit card balance get anywhere near your limit, the scoring model judges you as not being able to handle credit responsibly – period. Yes, you may be the exception, and you may have a valid reason why your balance is high, but your score doesn't care. It wasn't designed for your individual circumstances; it was designed to make billions of decisions about hundreds of millions of people.

This magical 'what you owe versus your limit' absolutely destroys your score if any card has a balance of more than half your limit. If that's you, even if you have around a mid-700's score, it'll drop 30–40 points, according to Fair Issac. If you owe more than 50% on your cards, getting the balance below 20% can increase your score in the same proportion. What's just as critical is that the scoring model calculates the credit utilization for each of your cards, as well as the totals of all of them. As a result, if your score matters to you, it's more important to first get all your cards below 50% before focusing on paying any one card in full.

Getting below a 50% balance just assures you that your score isn't negatively impacted. To boost your score, less is more. The old rule of thumb was to keep balances below 30% of credit limits. That isn't the case anymore. It's still the cut-off where your score won't be negatively impacted, but to boost your score it needs to be below 20%. A balance of less than 20% of your limit is the magic cut-off point where your score can grow significantly. Below that, FICO has found very little difference if your utilization is below 10% or 20%, according to FICO spokesman Anthony Sprauve.

A reasonable rule of thumb is that your credit score can't get to the magical 720 or higher if you have credit cards with a balance of 50% or more. Conversely, if your payments are made on time and your credit cards are less than 20–30% of their limits, it's likely your score will never drop below 720.

These four magic cut-offs, above 50%, below 50%, below 30%, and under 20%, come from spokespeople at Fair Issac, the developers of FICO scores themselves. There are some additional tricks or insights that will make a significant difference in boosting your score:

- Focus on paying down your credit cards. There's a big difference to your score when paying a credit card down versus paying a vehicle or fixed installment loan. Credit card debt is judged as a much higher risk. As a result there'll be way more impact on raising your score if you take extra money to pay down your credit card balance instead of a loan.

- Don't move things around. You'll need to focus your time, energy, and money on paying down your credit card balances, not moving the balances around. Moving to a lower rate card may save you some interest, but it won't help your score. In fact, it will likely make things worse. According to FICO, a balance transfer to a new card can drop your score 25–35 points if you already have a number of other cards. Conversely, if you only have one or two, it may help your score, but only by a few points.

A new card application will impact your score as it creates a new credit inquiry, and the length of your average history will also drop with a new card. A balance transfer will most often be to the full limit of the new card. So you now have a card at 100% balance versus limit, and that will do even more damage to your credit score. If you take any advice, never do the balance transfer request with the application. If you're requesting a $5,000 balance transfer, it's likely the new card issuer will simply give you a $5,000 limit. That's 100% utilization and will kill your score. Let them process your application, set the limit, and *then* decide the balance transfer amount.

- Be careful when financing a boat, ATV or motorcycle. If you're setting up payments on any of these through a dealer or retailer, be careful! Most of these will be set up as a revolving charge account. That makes them appear in your credit scoring the same way as a huge retail store credit card balance. Plus, it'll reflect a limit that is pretty much the same as your financed amount. Your credit score treats this like a credit card and scores it as a massive danger item because of your balance versus limit. Don't do it. Go to the credit union and get a fixed loan instead.

- Stay away from no-no plans. If you're tempted by a no interest or no payment plan, don't do it. These plans also set you up with a store credit card. While the savings may seem tempting, you're getting trapped in four different ways:

  - It's a store card that will drop your credit score for its inquiry.

  - You'll get it at or near the total you're buying, which massively drops your score because it'll be close to 100% balance to limit.

  - You'll be making no payments or paying very little if it's a no interest plan. That guarantees your score will say way down for the entire year since you're not reducing the balance significantly.

  - If you're payments are late any month, or when the plan ends and you still owe (even if you owe five cents), interest will be charged retroactively to day one for the full amount!

- Your credit card statement balance is critical. By the time you get your statement, it's too late to save your score. Your card issuers report only your statement balances to the credit bureau which trigger your score calculation. Yes, you may pay off the balance the next day, but by then, it's too late and the new balance will never be reported to the credit bureaus. Millions of people can never figure out why their scores aren't as high as they thought they should be, and that's the primary reason. To protect your score, you need to actually ensure that you don't use your cards for more than 30% of its limit in the first place! An alternate plan is to always make a payment a few days before your statement date. That early payment will be applied before the statement cut-off and will now report a much lower balance to the credit bureau, which can then increase your score.

- Try for a goodwill adjustment. If you've been a long time customer and have had only one late payment, call your card issuer immediately and ask for a goodwill adjustment. They may, just once, reverse the late report and late payment. Few things you can control on your credit score will matter more than that one call, as discussed in a separate section later in this chapter.

- Increase your limit. If you have a reasonable credit score already, there's a second way to get your credit card balances below 50%, or maybe even below 30%. It's through increasing your limit. If you have a $6,000 balance on a $10,000 card, your credit utilization is 60% and that will always be a major drag on your score. If the limit changes to $13,000, your utilization will be down to 46%. One call can instantly boost your score. But it shouldn't take away from your focus on paying down your balance because a $1,400 payment accomplishes the same thing. Just be careful because tons of people can get a high limit but few can avoid using it!

    Nothing in the five scoring factors cares about your total credit card limits. Your score won't change whether your credit limits total $100,000 or $5,000. It's only about the percentage you're using.

- Keep an old dormant card active. A credit card you haven't used for a long time still reports to the bureau. After all, it's still a valid card. However, it won't have the same impact or weighting on your score as an active card, according to a quote by Fair Isaac.

After a year or so, the importance that your score places on that inactive card is reduced. Having a zero balance card is perfect, but do pull it out every six months for at least a $20 charge to avoid it from being excluded from your scoring as dormant. Inactivity will stop the credit score from adding its limit to your credit utilization calculations. While it may not make much sense, a card that's used for a tiny amount will actually give you a higher credit score than a card with no balance.

- Do the math before closing a credit card. One of the most common questions is whether or not you should close a credit card and what the impact will be on your credit score. Unfortunately, there is no black or white answer. If you want to become debt free and non-credit-card-dependent, pay off the card and close the account. If, however, you also wish to protect your score, you'll need to consider a few other implications first. One of them is the length of that card's history, as discussed in the factors that make up your score.

The other consideration is that by closing a credit card it takes away its credit limit thereby lowering your credit utilization. If all your balances are less than 20% of your limits without this card, and if it's not the oldest card you have, and if you have at least two other cards, you'll be fairly safe that there won't be much (or a long) impact on your score. If closing it now jumps your balances versus limits over 30% or, even worse, over 50% – don't do it until the other cards are paid down first. Right now, you need that extra credit limit in the math formula that your score uses. Whether you close it or not, the history and past credit rating on the account will stay on your credit report for at least seven years. It will keep being used by your credit score calculations, just to a diminishing degree as time goes by. If you have other cards with a five-year or longer history, that's not much of an impact on your score.

> *Jacob was really ticked off by the incompetence and poor service of one of his credit card companies, and rightly so. For two months he took every dollar he could spare to pay off his $2,000 balance on his $5,000 limit card and closed the account. The following month he saw that his ok credit score had dropped by 44 points. His credit utilization had now increased because of the high balances to limits on his other two cards. The one he closed was the only one below 50% utilization. Now his score will stay low for a long time while he works on getting the other two balances below 50%. If Hugh had paid it off, but not closed the card, he'd have lowered his utilization and increased his score. Even better, if he had used the $2,000 between the other two cards, his score would have jumped above the magic 720 as all three cards would have now been below 50% utilization.*

No-limit credit cards will limit your score

Two types of cards can cause a major drop in your credit score, and it may come as a surprise to you. The first types are the *real* American Express cards. These so-called charge cards require you to pay the balance in full each month. Because they're charge cards and not credit cards they don't come with a fixed and formal credit limit on your statement. As a result, the critical credit score calculation in your credit score of balance versus limits can't be done! Your score can be permanently impacted by 30–50 points or more without a fixed credit limit, since credit utilization is the largest part of your score.

The second types of cards are those with no-limit where you'll probably always be near your limit. In the words of Craig Watts, spokesman for Fair Isaac, the developer of the score, "Consumers may want to think very carefully how deeply their scores will be affected." Chase, Barclays, and Bank of America, as one example, market the Visa Signature card with a supposed 'no present spending limit.' The marketing is that you won't have any over-limit fees. However, you do have a limit – it just isn't on your statement. As a result, any card with the supposed *no limit* will lower, or at least hold down, your credit score. All that the credit bureau can guess is that the largest statement balance you've ever had is your limit or high credit. If you regularly charge $2,000 a month and the highest you've ever been is $3,000, you'll always show as 67% utilization and you'll almost never get to less than 20%.

In order to create some 'room' between your typical balance and the high credit, try to run up some huge charges in a one month period. That will raise your highest credit amount and will give you that artificially high credit when compared to every subsequent month. If that one-time phony high now has your regular monthly charges at less than 20% of your so-called limit, you've maximized your credit score. If that can't be done, the only alternatives are to switch to a real-limit card, pay a large payment before your statement date, or curtail your use of the card. Remember that your credit score math does not know that it's a charge card and that you pay the full balance each month. It just keeps seeing a relatively small highest credit with a continuous high balance.

Devon and Kerry were turned down for their refinance, or told maybe they could get a subprime rate. All credit scoring, and zero common sense, meant nobody saw that they had a charge card which was negatively impacting their credit scores. When they discovered this, they faxed their last statement and receipt to their lender who rapidly re-scored their credit report. As a result of taking out this permanently maxed-out account, their score increased 76 points. Devon and Kerry immediately went from being turned down to obtaining conventional financing.

How lenders keep your score low

No matter what credit cards you have, you need to make sure that your credit limits are shown on your statement. In the past, a couple of card issuers became notorious for not reporting credit limits to the credit bureaus. Not showing the limits prevented other issuers from stealing their customers. But it also prevented the customers from ever getting their credit scores increased. When you always have close to 100% owing because the limit isn't reporting, your score is much lower than it should be through no fault of your own – and it's not even accurate! Make sure that your statement shows your limit by checking your credit bureau report.

In a perfect world for financial companies, you'd have a credit score that's good enough to have your credit application approved, but low enough where that they can maximize their interest rates. Not too low, because that increases the odds you'll default, but also not too high because they'd have no choice but to give you the best rates. That same speculation, and it's only that, can make you wonder if that's the reason credit bureaus really don't seem very motivated to fix credit report errors. After all, their customers are financial institutions, the ones who pay for credit reports and credit scores.

Some cards actually use a zero limit, or at best, correctly use the highest balance you've ever had any one month. Sadly, one of the largest issuers does not report even the highest balance on some types of cards. As a result, there have been documented examples of scores dropping between 35 and 50 points simply because the credit score constantly thinks the card is maxed out. According to the Office of the Comptroller, this type of reporting is allowed and a statement from one issuer, Citibank, explained that the "card agreement states that the customer has the flexibility to make purchases in excess of his/her limit. Therefore we do not report to the credit bureau the revolving credit line amount."

Previous Senate hearings actually had Capital One admitting that they often withheld reporting credit limits of their customers to the credit bureau, which resulted in lower credit scores being reported. Sallie Mae (the student loan giant) was also found to withhold positive information about student loans. Again, this negatively affects borrowers who are mostly young adults and already have fewer credit accounts, shorter track records, and now, much lower credit scores.

Think before you apply

Your credit score has a very good reason for dropping like a stone if you have a number of credit inquiries on your file. According to FICO senior scientist Frederic Huynh: "Statistically, people with six or more inquiries on their credit reports can be up to eight times more likely to declare bankruptcy than people with no inquiries on their reports." In an interview with the Boston Herald, Huynh goes on to confirm that shopping around for something does not count as a bunch of inquiries. There's always a window for multiple inquiries within a 30-day period. So it's perfectly fine to apply with three or four lenders if you're shopping around to refinance your home or getting a vehicle loan – and you should. In those cases, the one inquiry will impact your score by around five points. However, if you're shopping around for a vehicle loan *and* a HELOC *and* applying for a credit card, all three are different types of credit and will count as three inquiries!

As discussed in the credit card chapter, retail or department store cards will significantly damage your score. That 10% off you may receive today will also get you 5 – 30 points off your credit score. That's according to FICO's own statements, but depends on your credit score and how many other applications you've had recently. It'll be scored as a type of 'last choice of credit' because of the high interest rates on these cards. That damage can work its way out of your score within six months, but it isn't worth the trouble. Even if you take the store discount and immediately close the card, it's too late. The damage is done because you can't reverse the credit bureau inquiry.

You'll also need to be careful with a 'bill me later' offer. Any time you don't have to pay today, you're really applying for credit. Interest rates over 20% are one thing, but their impact on your credit score is the same as applying for a store card. With the inquiry hit on your credit score and the 100% credit utilization, your score can drop up to 50 points just to get a 90-day credit account. Instead of 'bill me later', choose the 'buy it later' plan.

If you're late – you're dead

> You can't live for a better past. The impact of a late
> payment on your credit score will stay with you for
> two to three years. After the fact, there's nothing you
> can do to reverse the hit on your score, but wait.

Absolutely nothing else will help raise your score more than a history of on-time payments. That protects and increases the biggest portion (35%) of your credit score.

According to Fair Issac, the impact on your credit score with your first 30-day late payment in the last few years will cause a drop of 60–80 points, if your current score is around 680. Even worse, if your current score is a great 780, it'll drop around 90–110 points. Your first missed payment, or a first collection on your credit file, are the worst things that can happen to your score following bankruptcy, foreclosure, or all your cards nearing their maximum.

The higher your current score, the larger the impact will be of your first late payment. The scoring model thinks you're a great credit risk who hasn't been past due for three years or more. So it's much more of a 'shock' to your score when you're behind for the first time in years. It starts to think (the predictive part of your score) that this is a new trend and things may get worse. For someone in the mid 600's, the drop will be a little less, because the system has almost built-in the odd minor arrears already.

25% of people have a so-called golden score of 760 or higher. What's their secret? Less than 4% of them have ever been late on a payment in the seven years that a payment history stays on their credit files.

Increasing your score up to 100 points

A year from now you'll wish you had actually started today to fix your credit score.

While you live in a world of instant everything, that's not the case for your credit score. At best, what you do today will show up in your credit report in two or three months. Since your credit score uses your credit bureau reports, it takes the same length of time to move your score. It should be your main motivator to be pro-active and to think ahead. If you're ever going to be applying for credit, a job, bonding, home or vehicle insurance, or many other things, your credit score can be a large factor in helping or hindering you.

If you're willing and motivated to move up your credit score, you can certainly do so. If you're around the 650 mark, it isn't unreasonable to set a goal of gaining 100 points. If you're already above 700, some of these steps could grow your score by around half of that. If your score is in the mid 700s or higher already, there is only marginal room to grow beyond a few points.

None of these 10 steps involve borrowing, or making things worse. Remember that your credit score isn't necessarily a going-broke, or 'paying a lot of interest' score. Purchase your current score or use one of the free sites discussed earlier. Whichever you choose, just make sure that you're using the same one down the road for an accurate comparison. As a bit of a recap, for the next year:

- Don't apply for any new credit. If you choose to ignore this, everything else you do will likely just offset the damage by ignoring this point. A new account application, the resulting new account, a potential new debt, as well as now having no history and track record on this new account, are four ways to damage your score, not help it grow.

- Don't do any consolidations or balance transfers for the year.

- Get up to date on your payments and stay current.

- Get all your credit cards balances below 50% of your limits. At a mediocre score, that step alone can boost your score by 50 to 100 points. Both extra payments, and not using your card as much as you have been, impact your balance.

- If you're already at less than 50% of balances, get them to less than 30%, and then below 20% of their limits.

- Don't close any zero balance cards. If you have any inactive cards, use them for a $20 charge twice in the coming year to assure they stay active and count in your credit utilization.

- Pay off or settle in full any open collection items. While they stay on your file for seven years, their impact on your score is drastically reduced after two years, and again at the three year point, and when the balance is finally zero (settled or paid).

- Correct any errors in your credit report. Address and employment information aren't part of your score, but incorrect accounts, arrears, missing credit limits and the like certainly matter.

- Challenge any incorrect collections. If you have collections shown on your report which are inaccurate, beyond the Statute of Limitations, or not reporting payments, dispute them with the credit bureaus. They'll have to verify the accuracy or remove them from your file, and that'll adjust your credit score.

- Wait. This is the biggest factor to increasing your score. True, it's something you may not be very good at. The proof may be your credit card balance (gotta buy it today) or the high vehicle payment (no money down seemed like a good idea…). Time is the magic healer and best way to increase your credit score. Any old bad item ages and becomes less of a factor over time while fresh updates show on-time payments and lower balances as you're making payments.

If you're under age 25 or have newer accounts, one year also adds a significant amount of additional history to your entire credit file, as well as to each individual credit card or loan.

In the next year you may also reach the magical three year mark. A previous bankruptcy, paid tax lien, foreclosure, collection, or judgment will stay on your credit file for seven years, ten years in the case of bankruptcies. However, time does cure a lot of pain. After three years, the impact on your score will be minimal and significantly discounted in your score calculations. Simply check your credit report for the reporting date and you'll know when you'll reach the three-year mark. Your goal should be one of the three great score levels of 700, 720, and 760 as outlined at the beginning of this chapter.

If you had a problem with your home

More than four million families lost their homes in a short-sale or foreclosure. Another million-plus beat the odds and were actually approved for some kind of loan modification. If either of those applied to you, here are the implications on your credit score, as first reported in the LA Times:

A short sale for someone with an excellent credit rating will drop a score 120–130 points. A short sale will not save your credit. Many scam artists on the web will sell you a different version of reality, but none of them are true. According to Tom Quinn, VP of FICO Scores at Fair Isaac in an interview with the Minneapolis Star Tribune, "The claim that doing a short sale is not going to hurt your score is false. It's inaccurate."

Walking away from the home before foreclosure and letting the lender have the house back will drop it 140–150 points.

Bankruptcy will drop your credit score 150 to 240 points and will impact you the most for the first three years.

Loan modifications, where the late fees and arrears are rolled into the modification, can actually raise your credit score. How a modification impacts your score depends on the lender and how they choose to code the reporting to the credit bureaus. They can:

- Consider you to be paying as agreed since the modifications revised the original terms, conditions, and payments.

- Consider you in arrears each month as your modified payments are less than the original terms and monthly payment.

Auto and home insurance

"Today, all major automobile insurance companies use credit-based insurance scores in some capacity."
The Federal Trade Commission

Yes, insurance companies use your credit score to set your auto and home insurance rates. Is it allowed? Yes. Under the Fair Credit Reporting Act, credit information can be used as a factor to set your premiums, and it's legal in 48 states. Whether it's fair, necessary, or appropriate is quite another matter.

According to an analysis by Consumer Reports, this method of calculating a driver's risk could end up costing you hundreds of dollars each year. The majority of insurance companies use your modified credit report from Fair Isaac, or ChoicePoint, while a few have developed their own internal scoring models. According to the Fair Issac insurance manager's comments to Consumer Report, their Assist insurance score is based 40% on payment history and 60% on credit limits and balances. In addition, they take into consideration the length of your credit history, types of loans, etc.

Some states limit the use of credit scores in insurance rates. A good rule of thumb they may use is that someone with a clean driving record and above average credit history can expect a 25% lower insurance rate. Conversely, a lower credit score, if used, will cost you a lot of extra premiums, not to mention that insurance companies can (and will) also use your score to cancel your policy. To add insult to injury, the Supreme Court has decided that insurance companies don't have to tell you that your rates are higher because of your credit score.

You may believe that your credit score should have nothing to do with your insurance costs. But it does and will continue to do so. Or, in the words of one insurance company: "Credit scoring tends to reflect a client's level of responsibility and behavior when it comes to managing their finances. Actuarial analysis shows a direct link between credit score and the frequency and severity of claims. By adopting this factor, we are able to more accurately rate individual clients by customizing rates and charging an appropriate rate for the risk… [Your credit score] is automatically applied to the calculation of your premium."

How did you score?

As promised with the quiz at the beginning of this chapter, here are the answers to whether any of these items are part of your credit score calculations:

Applying for any type of credit	y
Applying for credit but getting declined	y
Applying for overdraft protection	y
Arrears by someone you co-signed for	y
Authorized user on someone's credit card	n
Bad credit account beyond Statute of Limitation	n
Bankruptcy	y
Being a victim of identity theft	y
Borrowing from your 401(k)	n
Cell phone contract	n
Change in income (up or down) or job title	n
Checking your own credit report	n
Closing a credit card	y
Collection agency pulling your credit file	n
Corrections to personal information on credit bureau	n
Co-signing anything for anyone	y
Credit card issuers updating their files	n
Credit card transfers to lower rate card	y
Credit counseling	n
Credit monitoring	n
Credit utilization (percentage you owe vs. your limits)	y
Debit card usage	n
Debt settlement (on your own or through a company)	y
Defaulting on a pawnshop loan	n
Defaulting on a payday loan	y
Disputing an item in your credit file	y
Don't pay for six months or a year finance plan	y
Early termination of contract by paying penalty fee	n
Employment or employment history	n
Filing for bankruptcy	y
Foreclosure or short sale	y
Fraud alert on your credit bureaus	n
Freezing your credit report	n

Getting a judgment against you	y
Getting divorced or separated	n
Getting sued	n
Going past due on any monthly payments	y
Having a mortgage-free home	n
Having or using overdraft	n
Having your name on any debts after divorce	y
How much you pay a month on your credit card	y
Identity theft protection coverage	n
Inactive credit card	y
Increasing your credit card balance(s)	y
Increasing your credit card limit(s)	y
Interest rate on any account	n
Landlord pulling your credit report	n
Layaway plans	n
Length of time you've had your credit file	y
Marital status or getting married	n
Partner getting a new loan in his or her name only	n
Pawnshop or title loans	n
Payday lender loans	n
Paying off or paying down a loan or credit card	y
Pre-paid cards	n
Refinancing a loan	y
Rental agreements	n
Secured credit card	y
Shopping around for one loan in a month	n
Store (retailer) credit card application	y
Tax lien	y
Type of credit accounts you have	y
Where you live	n
Your total wealth or assets	n

Vehicle Financing: Choosing Some Shiny Metal over Debt Freedom

*The question to ask is not what kind of car you
OWN, but rather what kind of car you OWE on.*

Financing a vehicle is likely the second largest debt you'll ever have. It's also something you tend to borrow for over and over again, with pretty steep payments and a lot of interest to pay for something which keeps dropping in value faster than you can pay for it.

If you're fortunate enough to have $30,000 saved, and give that money to an investment advisor, what would you like to have happen? What if your advisor calls you in five years and tells you, 'Great news! That $30,000 is now down to $12,000!' How would you react when $18,000 of your hard earned money is gone and will never come back? How sick would you feel, and how quickly would you learn an expensive lesson that you'll never repeat?

Unfortunately, that's what millions of people do annually when buying a new vehicle. According to Consumer Report, even the best vehicles at holding their resale values, still depreciate 55% to 60% in the first five years. To make matters worse, one out of four people who sign up for this go-broke plan end up trading-in their vehicles before their loans are paid down, and owe an average of more than $4,000 over the trade-in value (according to edmonds.com). Left out of the above example was the interest cost. The story assumed that you were paying cash – and that's not the case for seven out of ten buyers.

The definition of someone's success should be measured by whether a vehicle is paid for and not whether it's brand new and financed to the hilt. In the first case, the person is financially successful, in the other case, the person is broke.

> *Even after signing a $2.2 million contract, Alfred Morris of the Washington Redskins continued to drive his 1991 Mazda 626. "One day, my kids are going to drive that car. If it breaks down, I'm getting it fixed. That's just how I am," shares Morris in a Yahoo Sports interview.*

Yes, you and most people would love to have fancy new vehicles with that new car smell. But neither one lasts for more than a month, while sadly the payments last for years. If you think about it, everybody actually drives a used vehicle. Until you have the financial resources to pay cash where you won't miss the $20 or $30,000, it's virtually impossible to reach financial independence while trying to juggle vehicle payments at the same time.

You can recover from overpaying $20 a month on a bad cell phone contract, or a one-year contract for a gym you barely remember. But, you can't recover from a five, six, or seven-year vehicle payment. The term is too long, the interest is too steep, the depreciation won't stop, and you cannot simply change your mind. Before you even start thinking of a new vehicle, go to edmunds.com. The site has an interactive section called True Cost to Own. Plug in the vehicle you're shopping for to calculate the total cost with interest, depreciation, insurance, and taxes at: www.edmunds.com – then go to: new cars – true cost to own.

In addition to all the interest and depreciation, remember that your new vehicle payments are made with after-tax money. So a $400 payment will eat up almost $600 of your gross pay.

Not having a vehicle payment, saving $200 a month by doing a budget, and temporarily increasing your income by $500 a month will give you an additional $1,300 of freed up money every month. How quickly could you become debt-free and financially independent with your current income PLUS an extra $1,300 a month?

Until you reach that point, stick with a used vehicle that you can afford and can pay for in cash. Think of yourself as being too smart and too successful to buy a new vehicle for at least the next few years. With that mindset, you can then start to feel sorry for those who do, and stop reading the rest of this chapter.

How much were you looking to spend a month?

There's the truth, there's fiction, and then there's automobile-speak.
Consumer advocate Phil Edmonston

On every car lot, at some point in time, every sales person will ask you that very harmless sounding question, '*do you want to just give me a blank check*'? If you're like almost every other person, you'll give an answer, and it can cost you a lot of money. Would you go into a dealership and volunteer, '*charge me whatever price, give me $1,000 of this and that fee, add some of that undercoating crap, and make sure it's a 10% rate on an eight-year loan*'?

Nothing suits a salesperson better than to have you focus only on the payment instead of the price. Let's face it; they would rather haggle over $10 a month, which might add up to $600 for a five-year loan, than to have you negotiate a $1,500 price reduction.

Plus, the dealer will almost always be able to accommodate your payment. After all, it doesn't appear to be important that the loan may be over five, six, or now even eight years in duration, or be a long-term lease or balloon contract, which now increases the total you'll be paying even higher. It's by far the best opportunity for dealers to mark up their rate, charge you a price others would never consider, and include additional charges and junk add-ons. All that, and your payment can still be exactly what you wanted!

If you're going to finance a vehicle, you will first need to decide what your priorities are: the lowest possible payment, or paying off the vehicle as soon as possible? The answer to that question matters a lot – and will cost or save you literally thousands of dollars in interest. Oh sure, you can now get an eight year loan – but is that how long you will actually drive that same vehicle?

Your lowest payment will always be your worst deal. Getting the payment down will necessitate stretching the term! Yet, only an extra 20 or 30 dollars a month can shorten your loan by about six months. It's a wonderful feeling when you drive the vehicle you love – but it's more important that you hate the payments that come with it, and resolve to get those over and done with as soon as possible – whatever it takes.

As with all your borrowing, always ask yourself:
is the price worth the cost? It might sound like
a simple question, but it isn't at all…

If you extend your term beyond four years, your payment will drop, but the interest you'll pay will skyrocket in direct proportion to the length of your loan. In fact, over a third of all vehicle financing is now for six years or longer. A small savings a month will massively increase your total expense. For an easy example, the following chart shows a $20,000 loan:

Term	Monthly payment	Lower p'mt per month	Extra interest	Total interest
4 years	470			2,560
5 years	387	(83)	660	3,220
6 years	331	(56)	612	3,832
7 years	292	(39)	696	4,528
8 years	263	(29)	720	5,248

It's the age old saying: You can pay it now (a little more each month), or you can pay it later (stretched out) but it'll cost you!

Financially successful people ask how much? People stuck in a lifetime of payments ask: How much per month?

Practice financing your next vehicle

There are few things better than making the last payment on a vehicle loan. Finally! All those years of payments and you're done. But how do you, and millions of other people, celebrate that milestone? By immediately going out and getting another vehicle, and likely for a higher payment on a more expensive vehicle.

In an ideal world you'd pay cash for your next vehicle. To get out of the permanent payment cycle, you'll need to drive your current one after it's paid in full. That will now free up the payment you had been making. Yet, since you can't be without a vehicle, at some point in the future you will eventually need to replace it. When you begin to think and plan ahead, you'll be ready. Until then, if cabbies can make their vehicles last for at least 300,000 miles, so can you… if you chose to.

Since your payments are now over, immediately have your bank take the exact payment you had been making and transfer that money from your checking account to a separate savings account.

You'll still be making the same payment, but now you're making it to yourself! Depending on what your payment was, you'll be paying yourself a huge amount of money and earning interest. Make it a game and not a pain, and you will permanently get yourself out of the vicious buy and finance cycle you can get trapped in for most of your life.

> *After five years, Karen finally paid off her Ford. She took the advice above and had her $360 payments re-deposited into a savings account. A year later, those 12 payments had grown to over $4,300 in her account. While she really wanted to replace her vehicle, she decided to hold off another year. Another year later, her savings had grown to $9,000 and she sold her Ford privately for $3,000. At that point she just couldn't bring herself to spending all $12,000, and just bought a $7,000, three-year old vehicle in cash. Karen went from permanent no-money down financing to paying cash, and still kept $5,000 in her savings. To this day she is still making the same $360 payments to herself, but they're going into investments that grow, and not into a vehicle that depreciates.*

Where to finance

It is critical that you slow down long enough to get the complete picture before buying a vehicle. You will need to get the total price of the vehicle, including the taxes and fees. Then obtain three quotes for your financing: one from a bank, one from a credit union (which will almost always have the best rate), and one from the dealership finance office. When you follow these steps, it will guarantee that you will not be sold an interest rate which has been marked up (inflated), or which isn't competitive with what your credit score ought to qualify you for.

Shopping around and buying has to be on different days. A small deposit marked 'subject to suitable financing' will always hold the vehicle so you can do your rate shopping. If the dealer won't hold it without a deposit, it's your best clue that it's probably an unethical dealer, a high pressure sales attempt, and not the place where you'll want to buy anyway. You have to remember that speed kills and convenience comes at a very high cost. If you want it fast, you'll pay. By not shopping around, it will likely cost you one or two percentage points, which can add up to more than $2,000 over the term of your loan. Since it's not likely that your income is more than $1,000 or $2,000 a day, going to two appointments to shop for your financing will pay off in huge ways. If you're Hispanic or African American, this advice becomes even more critical and is discussed in your own chapter.

Meet the business or finance manager

When you have found the vehicle you want to buy and you agree to the price, the sales person will send you to the dealership finance department. Their job is to take a deposit, get your financing, and sell a large variety of add-on after-market products, all of which have a huge mark-up, and none of which you need.

It's the responsibility of the finance office to ensure that all the legal documents are signed and that the sale actually goes through – no matter what it takes. Make no mistake, it is a large profit center, and for most dealers, this department makes almost half of the total dealership profits. The business manager is entirely on commission and understands the sales game much more than the financial field.

All the 2010 financial reforms and the powers of the
Consumer Financial Protection Bureau exempted auto
dealers. They do almost 80% of all loans through their
finance departments, and they were exempted.
All the rip-offs and traps from unscrupulous
dealers will keep going... and growing!

Whatever it takes, the finance manager wants to be involved in your loan. Only then are they able to sell after-market products, bump (increase) the interest rate charged, and sell insurance (that you should never buy) as part of the loan or lease. After all, it is much easier to sell you a $30 warranty (per month), than to sell you a $1,500 policy.

If you can trust yourself to not sign anything on the spot, you may get a head start in exploring your financing options by getting a rate quote that you can then take to the bank and credit union. If you get impatient, it won't be hard for them to talk you into just getting it all done right there – right then. But you'll likely be paying a steep price for the convenience to have someone set up your financing. It's like the convenience you pay for when you're eating in a restaurant. You know the actual ingredients cost 20–30% of what you'll pay for your meal, but you're choosing the convenience, ambiance, and service – at a price.

Bad news: You can take it home today

Dealerships know that buyer's remorse sets in about an hour or two after signing an offer to purchase. Somewhere around that time your 'what did I just do' wave of second-guessing can start. With door-to-door pressure sales, and even timeshare presentations, in most states you have a 48-hour cooling off period. This is not the case with a vehicle purchase, unless you do the most critical thing, which is to never shop and buy on the same day.

If you do not follow this advice, you're at the mercy of the dealer whose sole focus is to get your butt into the vehicle and out the door – no matter what it takes – as fast as possible. Only you can call a time-out. Dealers know they have a limited time to get you into the vehicle and over the curb (their lingo for taking delivery). That's why, more often than not, they'll simply roll or spot the vehicle to you. They'll have you execute all the loan documents, but if they cannot get the financing approved at the time, you'll be taking the vehicle home anyway.

There will be a problem with the financing the next day or the following week – bank on it. After all, automated approvals come in less than a minute. If it wasn't instant in your case, it's a big red flag that there's a problem. Later, the dealership can always get the vehicle back, or change the interest rate, the term, or your down payment. And you'll agree to the worse-than-original term and a higher rate 99% of the time. Why? Because dealers know that the more people that have seen your new vehicle, the smaller the odds are that you'll just return it if they can't get the financing done as agreed. At that point, you're trapped, you're committed, and now they can move the rate up, and you'll feel obligated to re-sign an entirely new loan agreement.

Do not let the dealer arrange the financing on the spot without shopping around. If you choose the expensive option of having them do the financing, never take delivery until the loan is approved. Plan C, if you ignore both of these suggestions, just return the vehicle if they cannot get your financing done on the terms you initially agreed to! If you just return the keys, you'd be amazed what they'll do to save the sale. Most likely, they will reduce your price to offset the higher interest rate or fees charged, that they are now trying to stick you with.

Don't let a dealer spot you the vehicle – ever. There's a good chance you will not get back any deposit you have paid, and your trade (if you had one) may have been sold, or just hidden, in an effort to pressure you into signing an amended contract. In this case, you'll get a lowball (actual wholesale) cash offer for your vehicle, and not the retail sale price.

Leasing made simple

Many states have little or no consumer protection on leases. They are a very bad idea for the vast majority of people, especially when you have no clue what the real rate, price, or buried fees really add up to, and you only focus on the payment.

A lease is an alternate way of paying for a part of your vehicle. It's the automotive equivalent of pay as you go cell phones. To reduce the higher monthly payments of a finance contract, a lease takes the future value of the vehicle out of the amount financed. It allows payment for what you are using and not payment on the entire vehicle. The part left out of the financing for the end is called the residual or buyout. On a three-year lease, the estimate might be that the vehicle is worth 40 percent at the end. On $20,000, that takes $8,000 off and charges principal payments only on the other $12,000. There will still be interest on the whole amount – after all you're driving the whole vehicle, but you are paying back only the $12,000 that you are using.

When the lease is over, the vehicle still isn't paid for. The $8,000 that was left out now has to be dealt with. It is your decision of what to do, and your choices at the end of the lease are to:

Walk away from the buyout balance – after all, if it's not worth that much, why would you want to pay it? Dropping off the vehicle does mean you will have nothing to drive and nothing to show for years of payments. You will also pay for any damage, missing equipment, and extra mileage, since every lease comes with a restricted amount of mileage.

Sell it or trade it – you still owe $8,000 plus the tax but anything more than that is yours (it is called equity – the difference between what you owe and what it's worth… just don't count on having any equity with the lease).

Refinance the balance to finish paying it off. A new loan takes the $8,000 buyout balance, adds the taxes, and finances this for another term.

You negotiate the price on a lease the same way you do on a purchase, and what you decide will affect your payment. The buyout at the end doesn't change – it is always a percentage of the sticker price. However, a lease is not like renting a car for a couple of months. You cannot simply return the vehicle before the end of the contract. It's called an early termination and will be very expensive to break. You have to be aware that:

- Interest is charged on the whole vehicle price, but you're never making payments towards the end-value (the reason for lower payments).

- A penalty applies on every mile you have driven over and above the contract mileage, including all excess wear & tear.

- The end balance, or buyout, will be approximately what it is worth – there will not be much equity, if any.

- At that time, you'll have another round of financing for the buyout and taxes, if you choose to keep the vehicle.

- Higher depreciation occurs with all vehicles in the first years. It results in larger total payments for a relatively shorter time on the road.

- There's a potential penalty as high as all the outstanding lease payments if you need to break the lease before expiry.

If you ignore the advice, or are currently in a lease that is due to be returned, you will need to do a little homework. Make sure you are within the mileage allowed, or calculate what the mileage penalty will be. If that figure is significant, you will likely have little choice but to re-finance the vehicle and to keep it, or sell it privately. Look at your lease agreement to get the amount of the buyout and then get an idea of the actual value in your market. Two places to start are at: www.kbb.com or www.edmunds.com.

Assure that any damage is repaired, including the windshield. It will be cheaper for you to get it fixed than for the dealer to repair it at their shop rate. Finally, make sure that you take a large number of pictures when you return the vehicle, including one of the odometer. The average charge for a lease return is $1,800 and you will want to protect yourself with pictures and a signed condition-and-return report! They are your only proof if there is a dispute or reconditioning charges down the road.

The last time I picked up a friend for dinner she actually started laughing and asked why I was still driving "this piece of crap," as she called my car. You see, there are two kinds of attitudes when it comes to vehicles, those who believe it's a status symbol and those who think it's nothing more than reliable transportation. My car is an eight-year old one that I purchased for $6,500 cash. Today, it's worth about $3,000, and has been trouble-free for six years, other than normal maintenance.

In the last six years my friend has had three leased vehicles – each one nicer than the last one. She's in the car business and gets the best deal, and even makes sure her lease payments never exceed $400 a month.

But tell me roughly when you'll have your utility bill paid in full? That's exactly the same as having a lease, and she'll have payments for the rest of her life – or until she gets out of the lease cycle of permanent payments. Her humorous comment turned to depression really quickly when I walked her through the math of status symbol versus basic transportation. Excluding her higher insurance costs, bigger gas bill, taxes, and maintenance, my 'crappy' car was $6,500 with a current value of about $3,000. It's cost me $3,500 to drive for the last six years. Her cool lease has been six years at $400 a month, which is $29,000 and counting. It's actually over $40,000 with taxes on the lease payments.

What's the money score right now? I'm ahead of the game by over $26,000. And today, her leased vehicle is worth $7,000 LESS than she owes, since a lease is never designed to build equity, but rather just to keep up with the depreciation (and it often doesn't even do that). That means at the end of this current lease she'll have nothing to drive and will either be taking the bus home or leasing again.

Careful if you get a car allowance

Do not let a car allowance be your great excuse and hunting license to get a new vehicle financed for that same payment. First and foremost, your car allowance is taxed, so you really have about

30% less than you're likely going to spend. Another trap is that your vehicle payments will not stop if you are to lose your job, take a position that no longer gets an allowance, or a host of other reasons. Your income will stop, but the payments won't. A car allowance reimburses you for the use of your vehicle. It doesn't say that the money has to be for a Mercedes or for a financed vehicle.

Don't join the majority of people who use a car allowance as a license to go shopping and into debt for something that plummets in value. There's a reason your company gives you a car allowance and not a car! Your employer knows they are way better off to limit their risk to a fixed amount of money each month, instead of giving you a vehicle that will keep decreasing in value, need constant maintenance and repairs, and is generally a money pit. Because, if they did that, they would really be writing a blank check, and that's the last thing they would want to do. You need to look at your car expenses in the same way your employer does.

When something has gone wrong

Last but not least, all contracts are covered by something called the doctrine of holder-in-due course. This legal wording simply means the company doing the financing of your vehicle is protected. If your financing is set up through the dealership, the lender who holds your contract has purchased it in good faith, and payments have to be made. No matter what dispute you have with the dealer or the manufacturer, from misrepresentation to faulty merchandise, or a host of other problems, the issue is not with the lender. They were not involved and do have a right to be repaid. You can certainly pursue any action that's available to you, but cannot stop making payments to the lender.

Credit Cards:
Charge Today – Pay Whenever

"It's hard to serve the Master and MasterCard."
Bishop Vernie Russell, Jr.

When the first credit card was invented about 60 years ago, it didn't really catch on that well. It was Diner's Club, and designed exclusively for restaurant charges. Frank McNamara, the creator, signed up fewer than 100 members from his first mailer, but two years later was billing out over one million dollars. The credit card business was firmly established forever. With the massive costs of setting up and administering a credit card program, plus a learning curve that realized millions of dollars in write-offs, it became obvious in the late 1960s that only two companies of any size would survive. From ads, they removed any talk about charge, debt, or debit. Chargex became Visa, and Master Charge became MasterCard. Both started to evolve into financial services companies instead of simple credit card issuers.

In the early days, banks actually had little interest in credit cards, but the current processing of billions of checks was very expensive. Credit cards became the bridge from the use of checks, to their eventual goal of total electronic banking. It was a training ground for you, or at least for your parents, to convert from checks to little plastic cards. It wasn't that hard to sell, and all that remained doing was a lot of marketing. If you keep hearing that you'll soon be living in a cashless society, the drive towards that goal comes from the credit card industry, and nothing would please them more. In fact, the last MasterCard annual report title was: A World Beyond Cash; while Visa calls itself: The Currency of Progress.

Credit card issuers market addiction under the guise of convenience. With the exception of HELOCs, almost all other borrowing sets up payments for a fixed amount and a specific term. With those loans, you'll always know there's an end in sight just by making the set number of payments. Quite the opposite is true with credit cards where your minimum payment won't pay off the balance for 20 to 30 years. And that's assuming you never charge another dollar!

Statistics from the Federal Reserve show that only about 30% of credit card holders pay their balances in full each month. That leaves millions of people trapped and broke paying interest rates anywhere from 10% to 80%. Yes, there really is a 79.9% credit card. It really can be the marketing of addiction. It almost never starts out as a problem by having one credit card, or the second card with a cool introductory offer, but for millions of people it can be just the beginning of a lifetime of trouble.

> *During college it was easier to stand in the credit card line than the student loan line and fill out all that paperwork, so I accumulated over $20,000 in credit card debt. That was OK at the time because I KNEW I would get a good job and be able to pay that off. In my twenties, I got married and bought a home. Soon, I was a thirty-something thinking I was doing most of the right things. My wife and I owned a home (with a mortgage), two cars, had three children, and credit card debt. We told ourselves that the credit cards were a necessary evil (we told ourselves at the time) and provided some cushion and convenience that we KNEW we would be able to pay off... someday.*
>
> *In 2008 I was off work for six months... more credit card debt. In 2009, my wife totaled her car... another car payment... Christmas for the kids, $400 here and there for car repairs, 0% interest for 12 months, a used car on a 0% balance transfer, restaurants, food and clothes, just to name*

a few of our expenses. As a forty-something, I was now staring down the barrel of more than $50,000 in credit card debt. It wasn't the amount of debt that was troubling me as much as it was the credit card companies seeming to deliberately work against me. Bank of America increased our credit limit to $25,000. When the 0% changed to 7.24%, it still did not concern us because we were making payments on-time, and knew it would be paid off someday. Then the interest rates began to climb even higher – to over 16%!

They weren't the only company there to 'help' us. Chase extended us a $13,000 balance transfer at 0%. Again, the 0% changed to 7¼%, but we also knew that it would be paid off someday. Then their rate began to climb to 13% in spite of on-time payments. Within a year, Chase closed the account on us. Our $25,000 Sears MasterCard began as an 'only for emergencies' card, and with an interest rate of 25% it's pretty easy to understand why. We had no intention of ever getting close to that amount but when we hit the $15,000 mark we knew we needed to stop using it. But we still knew that we would pay it off someday.

The final straw came when all three issuers reduced our credit limits because "balances relative to your credit lines are too high," even though we had never been late on any of these cards. The net effect, despite that we had paid down the principal balance by over $12,000 on those three cards, was that our credit report now showed our current balance was just slightly below our credit line, effectively destroying our credit score. We were trapped in a vicious cycle. No matter how much principal we paid, the limits kept getting reduced. This always showed us close to a 100% debt to limit ratio, which kept our rates high and rising, while plummeting our credit score. Were these card issuers intentionally stacking the deck against us? —E.M

The story does have a happy ending, continued in the Who to See and Who to Avoid chapter.

Credit card companies are not your friends

The unofficial mission statement of credit card issuers should probably be: Have your balance just below your limit, pay only the minimum payment each month on a card with a high interest rate and annual fee. They want you owing enough that you can never pay it off, but not enough where you'll go bankrupt and wipe out their incredible profits. If they need to throw in the odd free T-shirt, or other perks you'll probably never claim, so be it. They'll do whatever it takes to keep you owing, paying, charging, and broke, and being broke.

If you somehow manage to pay them off and get away from them, it's sad, but there are 2 billion 39 million other credit cards out in the world whose owners aren't as fortunate.

In the summer of 2011, a Federal Agency called the Consumer Financial Protection Bureau (CFPB) took over responsibilities due to the oversight of the credit card industry. Their first three actions and settlements against credit card issuers were:

Discover: A $214 million fine for deceptive marketing practices.

Capital One: A fine of $210 million, also for deceptive marketing of their credit protection products.

American Express: Refunds to 85 million customers for breach of consumer protection laws and a $27.5 million penalty.

That was followed in July of 2012 by Visa, MasterCard, and a group of banks, including Chase, Capital One, Wells Fargo, and Barclays, agreeing to pay $6 billion to settle a class-action lawsuit alleging they conspired to fix merchant fees at too high a rate. For the record, all of them denied any such allegations and claimed that they did nothing wrong...

At one hearing of the US Senate's subcommittee, testimony was given by three CEOs of the top credit card issuers and *also by Wesley Wannemacher of Ohio. Wannemacher used his Chase Bank credit card to pay for about $3,200 of wedding expenses. With a credit limit of $3,000, he was about $200 over his limit. During the next six years, he made payments totaling around $1,000 a year. Five years later he had paid about $6,300 on his original $3,200 balance. Yet he still had a $4,400 balance – $6,300 paid and he still owed $1,200 more than he started with five years earlier. Wannamacher, according to the subcommittee's investigation, was charged 47 over-limit fees totaling $1,500, and late fees of another $1,100.*

(US Senate Permanent Subcommittee on Investigations hearing: March 2007 – Wannemacher's balance was forgiven by Chase after he agreed to testify.)

If you want to watch a powerful video on the credit card industry, here's the link to PBS's Frontline: The Card Game at www.pbs.com – then go to: Frontline – search for "The Card Game."

Not all cards are alike

While there are almost 200 million credit cards in the U.S., there are essentially four different types of cards: major, charge, retail, and small business cards. They all let you charge something today and pay later, but the cards are treated very differently when it comes to how they reflect on your credit report and your credit score. (See those two chapters).

Major credit cards, also called bank cards, are Visa, Master-Card, American Express, and Discover. If you want to maintain an active credit score, and can trust yourself to keep the cards in your wallet or at home, the best rule of thumb is to have two of these major cards. It can be any two cards, or just two Visa cards, as long as they're from different financial institutions.

Your best credit card isn't a credit card, it's a charge card.

There's a difference between a credit card and a charge card, and it's something you need to know. American Express has lots of typical credit cards which provide a monthly statement from which you can pay anything between the minimum payment and the full balance. The original American Express cards are still around, but don't have the option of minimum payments. When the statement arrives, you have 21-days to pay the balance in full – period. You still do the charge part, just not the credit part beyond the grace period. If you want to assure yourself that you'll never ever carry a card balance, a charge card will do that. There'll be an annual fee, but it'll be worth it to achieve what you hope to accomplish, because there's no option of a minimum payment.

Your 2nd best credit card isn't a cash-back card:
It's a 'pay cash up front' card.

With your two major credit cards, there's still the question of what kind of perks or mileage card to have. Getting that free toaster is discussed in the next section, but the most common advice is to have a cash-back card. But – and the but matters a lot – don't lose your mind in ever thinking that you're getting free money, that you'll fund your retirement with this money, or that you're somehow getting one over on your card issuer. The purpose (if you choose) of having two major credit cards is to have a high credit score, free of charge, and free of charges on your card. You can have two credit cards, but almost all of your purchases should be with your debit card.

Even with the discipline of always paying your balance in full, the average credit card charge amount is 12% to 18% higher than paying cash. That fact is from an extensive study by Dun and Bradstreet some years ago. It's also something card issuers and every bartender, server, and retailer knows. When you pay by credit card, you'll tip more and spend more. Vending machines that accept credit cards increase sales by 178%, and one major fast food chain's average purchase showed an increase of 47% when paid by credit card. A credit card, just like chips in a casino, deceives your brain into thinking that it's not real money.

If you do carry a cash-back credit card and charge $5,000 a year for example, you're likely overspending to the tune of at least $600, because it's credit and not cold hard cash. No, you're not the exception – sorry. So even a 1.5% cash-back will give you $75… towards the $600 you've overspent!

Your last-best card isn't a retail store card.

The final type of credit card is a retail store card. These range from gas stations to department store chains, stereo stores, to furniture retailers. They are convenience charge cards to encourage loyalty to that chain's stores. After all, it's their card and you can't use it to shop at their competition. These cards are either operated by the company directly, or administered by large national firms.

For one national department store, upwards of half of all credit card charges are on their store card, and their employees receive bonuses and a lot of pressure to sign you up. Besides, 'you can get 10% off on everything you purchase today' if you apply for our card. You can bet that any retailer with an in-house credit card is really motivated to convince you to do that. After all, that discount offer will probably get you to buy something else (you didn't need), their sales and profits go up, and you're spending more than you would with cash. Now they just need one more thing: get you to not pay the balance in full – just once, and they're way ahead of the game. As well, you'll now come back more often because… well, you do have their store card.

Of the people who open a department store card with
a promise of '10% off today' – two-thirds are still
paying on the balance one year later!
Livingwithbadcredit.com

Whatever you do, whatever you're told, don't do it! You're trading a big drop in your credit score for a card with a 20–30% rate, a tiny one-time discount, and a drop in your credit score. If you're going to ignore that advice, check out the comparisons at Consumer Reports: www.consumerreports.org – then serch for: money – store credit cards.

What's THE best credit card available right now?

Do you want the information on the best credit card available? Here is a link for you at this book's website at: www.startfightingback.com and click on best credit card. The site will give you the card details, the direct phone number to the issuer, and the link to their application. The site is updated frequently, and is available exclusively to you as purchaser of the Fighting Back! book. (The password to this link will be the first word of a certain page in this book.)

Small business cards

You've probably noticed that large numbers of credit card ads now promote small business cards – whether you have a small business or not. That small shift in advertising has big implications and… surprise… it's not for your benefit. One card issuer's ad asks: "Why settle for less"? Don't do it – don't get one – ever. Another issuer simply asks you to tick a box on a personal card application by asking if you are a business professional with business expenses.

Don't fall for it, because they will issue you a so-called business card, instead.

The Credit Card Act of 2009 implemented a large list of consumer protection items by regulating credit cards. The law was drafted to apply to all credit cards, but small business cards were removed from the legislation at the last minute. What you have with a personal credit card that you do not have with a small business card is: the 21-day minimum grace period, a written notice before changes in terms and interest rates, payments applied towards your highest rate charges first, $50 maximum liability for fraud or card theft, refusal of permission to go over the limit, and no more retroactive rate increases.

You'll be enticed with some marketing stuff and a few more perks when you select the small business card. Why? Credit card issuers will gladly give up some tiny benefits to have you carry a card where they hold all the cards, and you have none of the consumer protection. With these so-called small business cards, they can go after you for any and all fraudulent charges if your card is lost, stolen, or used in an identity theft. Rate increases can still apply to your old balance and they can continue to apply your payments to the lowest rate charges first, to highlight just a few potential traps. Instead of taking the huge risks with these cards, get a personal credit card, use it only for business, and simply expense those charges for reimbursement.

All the downside and none of the upside –
all the traps and none of the benefits

One further heads up if you carry a business credit card issued by your company: there's a good chance that you're personally liable for your charges, even if the card is in the name of your employer. Before you take their card (or go back and check it) you need to read the disclosure on the application or their web site. You will see something along the wording of, "My company and I agree to be liable…" You may not think it's a problem today, but just ask vast numbers of people whose companies filed for bankruptcy, and card issuers started to come after them personally!

Perks and points – or a free toaster

One credit card has an ad featuring Alisha Keys in which a really dull guy becomes cool and popular when he gets this card. The card even allows him to hang out with Keys backstage. Unfortunately the disclosure whizzes across the screen before you can blink, in a font you'd never be able to read.

But the disclosure should probably say: "This is a credit card. It will help you with your going broke plan. It will not make you cool, nor is there any chance you'll meet Alisha Keys. This is credit card marketing and should not be confused with your real life."

Before you get excited about another credit card offer with the huge typeset of incredible perks, there are a few things you need to know.

First and foremost, any rewards card should only be used if you always, always, pay your balance in full. Most of these cards have annual fees and higher interest rates. If you don't pay your balance each month, it makes no sense to pay all those fees and interest in order to collect rewards, because you'll be paying out way more than you'll ever earn in rewards. If you want proof, about 60% of cards have a rewards program, but these cards account for over 80% of all credit card charges! Plus, almost all of them come with an annual fee. After all, you want some rewards, they want some (a lot) of your income first. Yes, many will waive your first year's annual fee. They're not being generous – they just want you to earn some points or miles first. After you've accumulated some perks, but way before you have enough to redeem, they'll start the annual fees. Now you're likely to pay the fee because, well, you're on the way to earning something... someday... maybe.

> *Sign-on offers and bonuses are loaded with traps and fine print. It's a safe bet that you won't read it (who does?), but only get excited about the huge font promoting the perks. Don't fall for it – what you see is seldom what you really get. Five percent cash back at department stores and restaurants! Surely that one is legit, isn't it? But read the fine print: "The accelerated cash back applies for a limited time." That time starts with your approval and is counting down while you're waiting for the card to arrive in the mail. When you get it, there may or may not still be time. The rest of the disclosure states that their five percent cash back applies only on the first $300 of purchases. In other words, the most you'll earn is $15! After that, it's back to the standard one percent. Oh, and if you don't spend at least $3,000 a year, it's 0.25%.*

Another popular card promotes 'up to 2% cash back'. However, the only words you need to read are 'up to'. When you go to the fine print, you'll see that it's 2%, but only in their stores, and only if you carried a balance the previous month (so they've already made 15% interest.) Everywhere else, it's not 2%, but 0.5%!

That free trip? You'll likely be grounded
You'll buy but you won't fly

Cash back cards can be redeemed for real cash that doesn't go bad, and it is something you can actually use. But the most popular cards are those offering airline miles. These miles can be earned on credit cards that most airlines market, but also on hundreds of other cards.

Airlines sell billions of miles in large blocks, mostly to credit card issuers, to give away as perks. American Airlines, as just one example from their filings with the Security and Exchange Commission, reported the sale of 175 billion miles to over 1,000 different companies. This was for their give-away in just one calendar year! That's great income for the airlines – not so good news for you. The reason is that there are almost 20 trillion airline miles earned and a lot of those people who want their free trip too. That helps to understand why Consumer Report found that over 75% of airline miles are never redeemed.

The consulting firm IdeaWorks did a study of what your odds are to book your frequent flyer ticket – and the odds aren't good. Their study found that US Airways, for example, could fulfill less than 11% of requests, and Delta less than 13%.

What are your points really worth… or costing you?

A pretty reputable dealership just started promoting '50 bonus miles' just to come in and take a test drive – and the promotion is going great! At a value of 1.2 cents a mile, shouldn't the ad state that they're offering 60 cents for a test drive? But then, who'd show up?

Each credit card issuer can use a different set of points or miles that you need to accumulate and redeem for different freebies. The best bang for the buck on airline miles is to actually attempt to get that free flight. To calculate what your miles are worth with different programs is not that difficult. The easiest way is to find how many points it will cost you to purchase a gift card for any retailer. Gift cards have a fixed value that cannot be inflated or messed with and a $100 gift card really is $100. If it takes 13,000 points to get the $100 gift card, you'll quickly know that each point you have is worth 1.3 cents.

As a rule of thumb, airline miles have a value of 1.2 cents. To redeem them for a flight is the real challenge, not only in getting the flight and the dates you want, but also in restrictions and fees that keep being added. To redeem them for anything other than a flight may not be as good a deal, but at least you'll get something for them. You can also check the website www.points.com for possible ways to redeem your miles or points towards restaurant gift cards, subscriptions, or even cash into your PayPal account. It'll be heavily discounted, so you have to read the fine print and know what the buy and sell restrictions are on your card or airline program.

Linda and Steve were never really heavy credit card users and most months they paid down, or even managed to pay off, their balances. Three years ago, however, they decided to get another credit card which offered airline miles, and decided to get serious about earning a long dreamed of vacation in England.

In order to speed up their point earnings, they started using this card for groceries and almost everywhere else that would accept the card. A night out with friends now meant Steve would get the cash from his friends, but put the whole restaurant bill on his credit card for the points. Magazine subscriptions were now charged, as was every tank of gas, trip to the mall, and everything else on the planet, in order to maximize their point accumulation.

Today, three years later, this card has a balance just below their limit, and Linda and Steve aren't even close to their free trip. What happened? Fortunately, the financial trail *can be traced because they kept copies of all their credit card statements. In the 30 or so charges a month, their brains stopped connecting a charge with spending real money. MRIs and brain scans have documented this over and over. When they used to pay cash for these charges, they were cognizant of pulling real $20 bills out of their wallets! The magazines were now on automatic renewal, something they didn't even notice, none of which they read much, and none of which they really wanted or needed. When dinners out with friends were charged to their credit card, Linda or Steve took the cash their friends paid towards their portion of the tab. What happened to that cash? Well, neither one could actually answer that – it just got spent...*

With at least a half dozen other questions and insights, Linda and Steve realized they made a big mistake. In the interest they've paid, the three years of $95 annual fees, the cash that leaked out of their wallets, the charges on the card they'd never have made before, and many other ways, chasing the free trip has cost them over $4,000 – and they're not flying anywhere...

If you believe that their story isn't one that plays out with millions of cardholders, you're mistaken. If you believe that this couldn't happen to you – you may be kidding yourself, and it may take another year or two before you realize it can or did...

*The only way to actually make money from
your credit card is to be a stockholder.*

If you're shopping for a reward card

If you are still on the lookout for a rewards card, you need to do your comparison shopping before sending in the application or submitting it online. Every issuer will run your credit report as soon as they receive your application. At that point, the inquiry into your report has already impacted your credit score. You need to first review a range of credit card offers to find one that isn't loaded with fine print and traps. Amongst many others, there are two web sites worth clicking when you're comparison shopping:

Bankrate has a number of search options by issuer, credit score, or types of cards. The site will also show you current interest rates, most popular cards (although you shouldn't care what others do), and a range of credit card calculators at: www.bankrate.com – then go to: credit cards – credit card calculators.

Want to find a card that will maximize your rewards or fits best with your spending patterns? Creditcardtuneup analyses what may best fit your needs of rate, rewards, etc. You should enter your current card spending from your last few credit card statements: www.creditcardtuneup.com.

Your credit limit & balance: know your limit – stay within it

All credit cards come with a pre-set spending maximum, which is your credit limit. Once every year or two, it's possible that you'll be offered an increase in your credit limit. That might seem flattering to you, but what your issuer is really trying to do is get you to charge enough where you can't pay off the balance in full. They still want to get paid back – just not very quickly. Remember that the goal of card issuers is to get the maximum number of cardholders to have balances close to their limits, with cardholders making at or near the minimum payments only.

When the economy is doing well the offers to increase credit limits accelerates. When the economy is doing poorly your credit limit can and may be lowered a little or a lot. Yes, they can do that. It's something millions of people found out the hard way at the lowest point in the economy in 2008 and 2009. With huge unemployment, and the massive drop in house values, card issuers got scared and cut credit limits from a high of $5 trillion down to about $3 trillion. Almost overnight, $2 trillion of available credit was cut with no notice, and quite indiscriminately. In fact, various studies have shown that these massive limit cuts were to over 95% of people who weren't past due or near their limits.

No matter what your credit limit is, it's imperative that you never exceed it. While most people think that it's a fixed maximum, that's not the case. Your card issuer will certainly let you go over your limit, but will charge you an average fee of $39. If you're caught being over your limit, a minimum payment the following month will only bring you just below the limit again. But being just below your limit, where new interest charges for the month will automatically put you back over your limit, will trigger another over limit charge. In other words, if you don't pay a lot more than the minimum payment, you'll pay fee after fee, month after month.

Fortunately, the new credit card laws specifically require your consent to have your credit limit exceeded. If you currently run a balance near your limit, or don't faithfully track your balance versus limit, you absolutely need to contact your card issuer to confirm that you opted out of their over limit charges. If you never charge anywhere near your limit, you should confirm that as well, just as a preventative measure. Simply call the number on the back of your credit cards: better safe than sorry.

If you want to ask for a credit limit increase, you'll need to do your homework first. Whether it's a higher limit or asking to have a previous limit cut restored, you will first need to check your credit score. While you're on the call, or when you press the send button online, your card issuer will immediately run a credit report update on you. A bad score, or a number of cards at or near their limits may well get your card cut off or the limit reduced further.

Your credit card interest is way more than you think

Your best rate is zero percent – and you get it the day you pay off your balance!

One of your best investments is always paying off outstanding debt, since the real cost is significantly higher than you realize. Since you don't have a choice but to pay income tax, you can only pay your credit card with your after tax net pay.

If you're able to save a little money each month by paying yourself first, you might be happy with a 7% to 10% return on your money. But how appealing would a totally risk free and guaranteed return of at least 22% be? Anyone with a credit card balance can have that return. To calculate your real cost of interest, simply take one minus your marginal tax rate, then take the rate of the card and divide it by that figure. For example: 1 – 0.25 (your tax bracket) = 0.75. Thus, your 19% credit card interest divided by this 0.75 is actually 25.3%.

At a 14% interest rate:		At a 19% rate:
In a 15% tax bracket	16.3%	22.4%
In a 25% tax bracket	18.7%	25.3%
In a 30% tax bracket	20.0%	27.1%

Why is the actual rate massively higher than shown on your statement? Because you need to earn more than one dollar to pay one dollar in debt after tax! You actually need to earn $1,334 gross, have your taxes taken off the top, in order to have $1,000 to pay if you're in a 25% tax bracket.

> *Card issuers would really rather talk about perks and points instead of interest rates. These items are cheaper to offer than having to reduce their rates and give up a whole lot of profit. Yet, it never hurts to ask for a rate reduction. A study by the U.S. Public Interest Research Group asked a wide range of people to call their card issuers and request a rate reduction. More than half actually received a lower rate just by asking. After all, if you don't ask – they won't volunteer it, but they sure want to keep their good clients, so make the call.*

Want to cut your interest by 60% or more?

Who wouldn't? You really can, and it's not difficult. You simply need to start making bi-weekly payments on your credit card. Unlike fixed loans such as your vehicle, the interest on your credit card balance is calculated daily. Paying every two weeks has you paying 26 times a year instead of 12. Here's an example: if you owe $5,000 on a credit card at 17% and have a 3% minimum payment, paying the minimum payments every month would cost you $4,000 in interest. You'll pay back $9,000 in just over 13 years! Instead of sending this month's minimum payment of $150, pay $75 every two weeks. It quickly adds up, your interest is reduced by over $2,500, and the balance is paid off in three years.

So stop charging and start paying. From now on, make things better, not worse. Want the whole thing over with even quicker?

It's just as easy – simply fix your monthly payments. On this $5,000 example at 3% minimum, your payment this month would be $150, but the 3% minimum payment will be a little less next month, a little less the month after that, and so on.

If you don't keep dropping these payments by a buck or two, and just stay with the $150 you paid this month, you've fixed your payments. As a result, more and more money from each payment will go towards the principal. If you do, the balance is paid in 46 months, instead of 13 years, and the interest paid drops from $4,000 to less than $1,900. You haven't paid a dime extra, but you're done with this card nine years earlier and at $2,100 less interest!

Take two minutes and test it with your actual balance and minimum payment this month. In less than a minute you'll become a believer by using almost any online calculator!

Credit card 'protection'

Credit card issuers bombard you with a range of offers to insure or protect you or your credit cards. Whatever they are, your response should always be: no way – never, ever. One card issuer recently sent out blocks of statements with a box already pre-ticked that just needed a signature on the payment slip. According to Fortune Magazine and a host of other media outlets, what many (or most?) people didn't realize is that they were signing up for a fee-based credit monitoring service called Watch-Guard Preferred at $72 a year! If you signed this without knowing what you were getting, contact them to get the $5.95 a month cancelled, but realize that you will likely only be refunded the last two months of charges.

Here are some of the common offers and easy explanations:

- Credit card fraud protection. According to the General Accounting Office, over $2.5 billion is collected each year by credit card companies selling card protection. However, they pay out less than 20% of this amount in actual coverage. In the insurance industry, the average payout is 80%. According to federal law, your maximum liability is $50 – period. And most card issuers don't even charge the $50.

- Life insurance protection. A Wall Street Journal exposé pretty much considers credit card life insurance to be the worst rip-off in the credit card industry. The coverage pays off the balance if you die, so you're really buying and paying to insure them and not you! And the coverage comes with some huge premiums. On a $5,000 balance, the premium can be up to 50 times higher than a term life policy. In other words, to protect the credit card company from a $5,000 loss, you could have bought a $250,000 term insurance policy for your family.

- Accident or sickness insurance. What you may not realize, unless you read the full disclosure, is that their super-expensive premiums for accident or sickness insurance will only cover your minimum payments. You pay all those premiums, and the average time off work is only around three months – and the issuer makes only the minimum payments! That leaves you back at square one when you do go back to work since all they've done is essentially pressed the pause button.

Check your statement:
What you don't know will cost you

According to the Wall Street Journal, a number of card issuers are now adding some kind of insurance coverage without consent or notification to the cardholder. The coverage shows up under some non-descript name that you probably won't recognize, but you'll need to challenge and reverse it, if you want it eliminated.

Whether it's your bank, cell phone, or credit card statement, you have to look through it each and every month. True, most people say they do, but they really don't. At best, six or seven percent of people do. Mistakes can happen and incorrect charges can end up on your credit card or bank statements. If you catch them within 60 days, you can get them reversed and credited back. Unfortunately, that's the maximum time limit before you're fully liable. By law, you only have the two months to dispute an error – any error, or you're paying – and that can be very expensive. The error or incorrect charge may be a one-off that's easy to dispute, or it may be an automatic monthly charge on your account.

One of many horror stories that received media coverage was from the LA Times consumer columnist David Lazarus. It detailed the story of a Bank of America client who was charged over $4,000 for something called Credit Protection Plus. The story is at: www.articles.latimes.com – then go to: business – search for "Bank of America should just play" – David Lazarus's column is worth bookmarking and visiting frequently.

In addition to misguided or misleading marketing attempts, crooks also count on you not checking your statement or disputing a charge you don't recognize. The FTC recently shut down a fraud ring that had been operating for years, based on that knowledge.

The crooks, using stolen credit card information, were processing charges on these cards. But the charges were always for small amounts ranging from a few cents to under nine dollars. They managed to keep their fraud going for an extended period of time on more than one million credit cards. How does the FTC know that only about six percent of people check their statements? According to a Yahoo! story, out of 1.3 million cards, that's the percentage of people who even noticed the phony charges.

Cheap temporary rate offers… sort of…

With average credit card rates over 14%, zero or close to it seems a heck of a lot cheaper… for a while. With low or zero temporary interest rates, millions of people spend a ton of time and energy moving their higher rate credit cards to an introductory rate one. It is commonly called credit card surfing. But what's the plan here? To save a few dollars of interest? And then what? Surf it over to another card in a year? All the moving around doesn't pay off a dime worth of debt. At some point in time, you need to acknowledge that you have a big credit card balance and actually get on with re-arranging your financial priorities to pay off the debt, not simply shuffling it around one more time.

What makes things worse is that, subconsciously, you tend to now think of this zero percent debt as not being real, or certainly not something you need to pay off very quickly. After all, it's interest free! So when the studies show that less than 25% of people pay off the balance during the zero percent period, you know it's true. It would seem silly to pay anything but minimum payments… and another year comes and goes… with you staying in debt…

Whether saving a few hundred dollars is worth it, is up to you. If you do decide to card surf, the card issuer has already won.

They're still profitable and have accomplished their number one goal of getting your balance way up there. In addition, you still risk going over limit, or your current or new card is now at or near the limit, and both of these have massive implications on your credit score. Plus, it'll keep your credit score lower for the entire year because you're probably not paying anything but minimum payments. Instead of saving a few dollars, there's a guaranteed way to pay zero percent interest: pay off your current balance and don't spend the time and energy in transfers in and out, back and forth. You're just kidding yourself that you're making progress – you're not. You're simply moving your debt from one place to another.

A recent caller to a financial-type talk show spent five minutes explaining how he made money on his credit card rate offer. He claimed it was a great deal to utilize a zero percent temporary credit card offer. He used his full $5,000 limit on the zero percent offer and put that same amount into a one-year CD at 1.75% making all that as profit. At the end of the year, he cashed in the CD and paid off the credit card.

If his card issuer was listening, they would have been proud, since all their marketing and junk offers were working exactly as planned. The caller, however, forgot to take four things into account. He:

– spent $150 on the balance transfer fee (since he mentioned the card offer, it wasn't hard to double check).

– only made $87.50 interest on the CD, but that was taxable. Even in a 20% tax bracket, the net would be $70 or less.

– had a maxed out credit card, which dropped his credit score significantly.

– gambled 12 months in a row that he wouldn't have late charges or over-limit fees as either one would have immediately canceled the promotional rate.

The final actual score: he lost $80 and at least two or three hours of work and trips to set up the CD at his financial institution. Even if there hadn't been the $150 balance transfer charge, was there a point in making $70 in a year with all that risk and drop in his credit score? Please! Sometimes the smartest people really do do the dumbest things.

One more thing you should know

Getting a credit card after bankruptcy or from a collection agency...

If you get a credit card offer from the same issuer that was part of your bankruptcy, or a collection agency offers to set you up with a new card, carefully read and understand all the fine print.

You may have a section in the disclosure where you are now reaffirming your old debt. In other words, you'll get the new credit card, but you've given your consent that the old collection, or charge-off in the bankruptcy can be put on this new credit card. They can't legally collect the charge-off from you, but you can give your consent to bring it back alive – and you do with some of these applications. It makes the old debt which was discharged, or way past its Statute of Limitations to collect, perfectly valid again where they can now pursue you and sue you for it.

Closed or inactive cards

Terminating a credit card is more than just putting it away, but that should definitely be the first step. The card is still perfectly valid and continues to stay active and alive.

If you choose to maintain a good credit score, keep two of your highest limit cards open and alive. In order to keep them active, they do need to get used, or they won't be much of a factor in your credit score. Use the card twice a year for a small charge. Many issuers are now setting minimum transaction amounts, but a $20 or $30 charge twice a year should be sufficient to keep it counting as an active card.

If you're done with credit cards and wish to close a card, the issuer must be notified. Whether the account is paid off or not, mail a note to your issuer asking for the account to be closed, and request a confirmation to be sent to you.

If you've consolidated or refinanced your debts and included your credit cards, you need to make a critical decision. Two-thirds of people have their consolidated credit card balances back up to the same amounts in less than two years. At that point you have the refi or consolidation payment and your credit cards are run up again. It's a huge recipe for financial disaster. If you do consolidate, close the extra cards, irrespective of the temporary small impact on your credit score. It's a small price to pay to avoid a worse financial nightmare down the road.

Prepaid cards

While these are often called prepaid *credit* cards, none of them have anything to do with credit. You're buying a piece of plastic with a magnetic stripe and paying cash up front that you can then use in stores and ATMs. They don't help to build or re-establish credit and they don't report to the credit bureau – never, ever. They're not a credit product, only a cash alternative, and a very poor one at that.

With recent stronger consumer and financial legislation, credit card issuers and others have turned their marketing towards prepaid reloadable debit cards. These cards are the main avenue banks use to strengthen their relationships with younger people. That's especially true for students who face large obstacles in obtaining a credit card on their own until age 21. The issuers' focus is also on lower-income people, and those who have no current bank relationship, or the so-called under-banked. A lot of marketing, little regulations, huge fees, and bad disclosure make it an attractive area of business. But it's working, since Americans load over $200 billion on these cards every year.

If you have a bank account, stay far away from pre-paid cards and get a proper debit card hooked to your bank account. For anyone without a bank account, like teenagers (make that parents of teenagers), prepaid cards can seem like a good idea, but be careful, because they are heavy on fees and light on consumer protection. It's critical that you shop around since the fees can be numerous and staggering. You also need to remember that pre-paid cards don't have the same fraud protection as credit cards. If your prepaid card is lost, stolen, or fraudulently used, you are liable for the loss, although some issuers do have their own voluntary guidelines. Fees that vary widely include:

Activation fee amount. Most cards charge to get the card set up and activated. The Walmart Money card is one of the cheapest at $3.00 with a lot less fees, but others can charge up to $45.

Cash advance fee. All cards will charge you a fee to get a cash advance from an ATM. As a result, you need to commit to never using the card to obtain cash.

Monthly fees. Most will charge a monthly fee. Why? Because they can, and they want to make a profit.

Balance inquiry fee. If you can't wait until you can get online, almost all cards will charge you for a balance inquiry through an ATM. That fee can double or triple with the fee the ATM provider will charge on top of it.

Number of months before inactivity fees start. You'll need to know when their inactivity fees start, beforehand.

Inactivity fee. You need to know when this kicks in. It can be over $10 and that kind of steep charge will quickly wipe out your balance.

If you're not that excited about a bank prepaid card, you can also get them from a large number of other companies or even people. How about a Justin Bieber prepaid card? Why? Because he wants to make money, and his 30 million Twitter followers and 53 million 'friends' on Facebook are just the right demographic – or they have parents who can buy the card. Sorry, but his fees are pretty steep compared to others, according to CardHub.com. If not Justin Bieber, there are many others, including a Suzie Orman The Approved Card. What's there to *approve*? It's your cash up front... does cash sometimes get rejected? The Rush card has 17 fees, Little Wayne's card (who knew there was one?) has seven, to name just a few more. You no longer have to look for the Kim Kardashian card. It was pulled pretty quickly after the Connecticut Attorney General started asking questions about her significant fees.

What are some cards with the least amount of fees? The U.S. Bank Convenient Cash Card and American Express Bluebird are two great choices. For a comparison of more than 80 cards and a personal calculator of fees based on your needs and usage, go to www.nerwallet.com/prepaid.

If you have a problem

One day – sooner, rather than later – you and every fellow American who has a credit card will have a problem or dispute. At that point, you'll be forced to call your card issuer's customer non-service department – sorry, but you don't have a choice. However, it doesn't need to be as stressful as you may think if you just remember a few points:

With your first call and with every call, always write down the date and exact time you called and the name of the person you spoke to. You cannot hold them accountable in your second or fifth call if you cannot rattle off all the names, titles, and dates. If you do make a written record of your calls, you can be sure they'll take you very seriously as they know you're taking notes and not going away until the matter is resolved to your satisfaction.

You only have 60-days to dispute a charge and have it taken off your statement. If it's for something you didn't buy, order, or want, you don't need to prove that a charge wasn't yours. After all, you cannot prove a negative. By law (they're not doing you a favor) your card issuer has to reverse the charge. They will contact the merchant for verification and if it was legitimate and signed for, they can re-post it to your account down the road. This 60-day time window is also the critical reason to never give anyone a deposit for anything that can't be done, bought, used, delivered, or fixed in that time period. If it doesn't happen within two months of the charge date, you cannot fight or dispute it later.

Do not send your credit card company a bunch of documentation. It isn't necessary by law, and just has them questioning you more. They may accuse you that this or that is missing so they can simply avoid reversing the charge, or they may try to just make you go away and give up.

If you're disputing a charge, fighting a limit decrease, reversing a rate increase, or disagreeing with one of their many fees, never threaten to close the account. Your understandably frustrated comment may be true and you should probably do so. However, during the calls, doing so will only kill their motivation to keep you as a satisfied customer. Stick with the theme of being a loyal customer and needing their help, please and thank you. Threats or frustration with someone handling hundreds of angry calls a day gives away all your power to negotiate. Get it fixed – then get away. They won't miss you, don't care, and you can do without them.

If you have a complaint about your card issuer

The Consumer Financial Protection Bureau now has an online database to register complaints against card issuers. The complaints will include disclosures of how issuers handle the complaint, but your information will stay confidential. Card issuers have 15-days to respond and 60-days to actually address the issue – and a complaint with the CFPB is something they take seriously. In the year prior to the online rollout, the agency had already received 16,000 complaints! To file a complaint online, go to: www.consumerfinance.gov.

If You're Hispanic
or African American

African Americans are 3.2 times more likely than whites to be jammed into a high-cost conventional loan and over 2.5 times more likely to be denied credit. Hispanics don't fare much better in that they are 2.6 times more likely to be steered into a high-cost conventional loan, and denied credit 2.3 times more than whites.
HMDA study by the Federal Financial Institutions Examination Council

If you're African-American, Hispanic, or almost any other minority group, the above excerpt is something you may have seen first-hand. Some of you know from friends and family who have been there and experienced it. It's sick, wrong, illegal, and it happens every day. The odds are overwhelming in that you'll get discriminated against in interest rates, down-payments, being wrongly denied credit, or steered into a subprime loan. The studies and lawsuits to prove that would fill an entire library.

Some years ago, the Harvard's Joint Center for Housing Studies came up with the median credit scores: Whites – 738, African Americans – 676, and Hispanics – 670. While that study is a few years old, the spread in scores is just as valid today. In fact, while the last recession plummeted the scores of millions of people, minority groups were hit even harder, which makes it fair to estimate that their median scores are even lower (worse) today.

With a lower credit score, it becomes easier for unscrupulous lenders to overcharge you in fees and rates. However, not all higher rates are discrimination. Charging you a higher rate because of your lower credit score is perfectly legal if that higher rate is charged to everyone else with a similar credit profile. In that case, it becomes even more important for you to know your score, and take the steps to move it up.

Never sign quickly or go quietly

While it often starts because of a lower credit score, why is the lending discrimination against you so widespread? You may be judged as being less informed, or just more trusting. In vast numbers of cases, it can also be your strong faith that has you believing others do have your best interests in mind, or that a broker or sales person is more trustworthy than they are. Your impatience in wanting to get the purchase and financing done quickly can also make it easier for someone to take advantage of you. Perhaps English is your second language, or you may be perceived as being easier to intimidate by credit jargon.

Hispanics now number about 51 million people in the country with over $700 billion in disposable income. The time has come to stop turning the American dream into the American nightmare when it comes to borrowing options, simply because English is not their first language. Hispanics are some of the hardest working people who, by nature are very trusting, often rely on word of mouth for referrals, and count on the honesty of lenders not to mislead them, or to take advantage of this trust.

You speak English, and perhaps Spanish, but you don't speak credit. When it comes time to understand what you're being told, or read the disclosure documents, you, just like most people, never do. And when credit people talk, it's as though they're speaking a language you've never heard. Sure you know the words, but when there are phrases or clauses you don't understand, you often don't ask. After all, nobody wants to look uninformed or stupid, but that can cost you a lot of money down the road, after it's too late to ask, or reverse your decision. If you're Hispanic, often seeing a sign that says, "Si hablo espanol," is simply Spanish for 'we can rip you off in your own language'!

Don't let anyone make you feel like English is a foreign language! Know the questions to ask, get informed, and know what you're getting into. Those three steps will save you a lot of money *before* you ever sign anything. Not getting the information up front is the same as playing a card game for money where you don't know the rules. Would you do it? Of course not! You'd be nuts to, and would spend a lot of money needlessly. The goal of sales people and lenders is to sell to you at the highest possible price, and to have control of the financing where you won't go anywhere else to comparison shop. Then it's to lend out the most amount of money at their highest rate and for the longest term. That's how they maximize their profits! Your job is to shop around, understand what the costs and fine print include, get the best deal for yourself, and to shorten the time you'll owe the money.

In the summer of 2012 the Department of Justice reached the largest fair lending settlement in history to resolve allegations that Countrywide Financial and its subsidiaries engaged in a widespread pattern or practice of discrimination against qualified African-American and Hispanic borrowers in their mortgage lending. It provided $335 million in compensation to these victims.

The settlement stemmed from the department's complaint which alleged that Countrywide discriminated by charging more than 200,000 African-American and Hispanic borrowers higher fees and rates. It alleged that these borrowers were overcharged because of their race or national origin, and not because of the borrowers' creditworthiness or other objective criteria related to borrower risk. Or to put it another way: if you were African-American or Hispanic, you were twice as likely to be jammed into a subprime loan compared to a white borrower with the same credit and income profile.

The Equal Credit Opportunity Act makes it illegal for any lender of any product to discriminate against you because of your race or color. This includes:

Refusing to grant you credit if you otherwise qualify.

Discouraging you from applying for credit in the first place.

Giving you credit terms, such as a higher rate that is different from someone else with similar creditworthiness.

You can file a complaint against any credit grantor through the Consumer Financial Protection Bureau at: www.consumerfinance.gov.

Before you need to file a complaint, there are seven basic steps you can take to protect yourself against lending discrimination.

Always get three quotes

The only way to be reasonably sure that a broker or sales person is giving you the best deal is after you've shopped around and educated yourself. It will give you a much greater level of self-confidence that you are getting a fair deal when you have one or two comparison quotes. Integrity is a core value for most people. Unfortunately it is not shared by everyone who is on commission, gets bonuses, or works for many questionable mortgage brokers, dealers, or lenders.

Just one of many examples where a second quote would have prevented an incredible amount of hardship is from the City of Baltimore. While these are all allegations which have not yet been proven in court, a lawsuit alleges that African-American applicants were told by Wells Fargo staff that they only qualified for subprime loans. According to one affidavit by a former loan officer Tony Paschal, even those who qualified for prime-rate mortgages were given subprime loans. "I had access to Wells Fargo customers' loan records and applicants' files… and regularly saw minority customers who had good credit scores and credit characteristics in subprime loans who should have qualified for prime or FHA loans."

Another former staff member testified that the company gave bonuses to loan officers who referred borrowers to the subprime division, who should otherwise have qualified for prime-rate loans. The lawsuit also alleges that the company targeted African-American churches to market subprime mortgage loans and that 69% of foreclosed homes are in primarily African-American neighborhoods, versus 16% in largely white areas.

(Mayor and City Council of Baltimore vs. Wells Fargo Bank, N.A. and Wells Fargo Financial Leasing, Inc., Civil No. JFM1: 08CV-00062, U.S. District Court for the District of Maryland)

Never buy or finance the same day as you're looking and shopping

Speed kills. That saying is true on the roads and applies to your financial decisions as well. The faster you want to sign the financing, the less time you make in order to take a deep breath, consider your options, to comparison shop, or to be aware when you're getting jammed into a bad deal.

Good deals are like buses: another one will come along right away. When everyone involved in the process from the sales person, broker, or finance manager knows that there is no chance you will be going from shopping to buying and signing on the same day, it becomes almost impossible to rush you or to overcharge you. At that point, everyone is aware that you will double check what they're telling you. That alone gives you incredible power, and gives everyone involved in the deal a heads up that you'll catch whatever they may mislead you about.

Get it in writing

A sales person or broker can tell you anything you want to hear, none of which needs to be true. The only thing that's legally enforceable is what's written in the contract or bill of sale. Never rely on any verbal promises, any 'we'll take care of that later' or 'we don't need to include that in the contract'. If it is not in writing, it didn't happen, and it isn't true. All your 'but they told me...' or 'they promised... they guaranteed me that...' is meaningless if it is not in writing.

You don't know what you don't know

How many times in your life will you buy a house or a vehicle? Five, six, maybe seven times? Mortgage brokers and finance people probably average that every day of every week... for years. After two years in the business, that makes the 'experience score' about 12,500 to 5! You may think you know what to avoid, ask, or do, but if you're wrong, you're voluntarily signing up for the stress, collections, and financial hell that's sure to follow if you're wrong.

Admit to yourself that the financial world is a minefield of tricks and traps, and that you don't know all the options or all the really important questions to ask. It'll make you more careful and slow down the process where you can get informed and not just get sold. If you choose to act like a know-it-all, you could have it all: overpaying, extra fees, inflated interest rates, and much more.

If you believe that it couldn't happen to you, you are being naive. Literally millions of people who have been part of class action lawsuits for discrimination and predatory lending all felt the same way, and were all very wrong – and way too late.

Subprime rates should NEVER be your first option

Subprime interest rates are often double, triple, or more than conventional rates. They're charged (or are supposed to only be charged) if your credit score is below a lender's cut-off point, a point where they believe their increased risk requires a higher rate.

Consumer groups and experts agree that many people could have avoided paying subprime rates by shopping around. In fact, during congressional hearings, one of the major subprime lenders disclosed some internal information: more than 19% of their clients actually had a credit score of 660 or higher. At that score, subprime rates should never have been charged! This lender also testified that this group included more than 30% Asian/ Pacific Islander borrowers, 23% Hispanics, and 12% African Americans. Another 22% of people had scores from 620 to 660, which also doesn't make subprime rates automatic.

In the words of the Center for Responsible Lending: subprime lending was designed for those who do not qualify for prime loans, but it is turning out to be used in vast numbers for

Hispanics and African-Americans, and very often in cases where they would easily qualify for prime loans.

> *African-Americans are over four times more likely to end up with a subprime mortgage loan, and on FHA backed mortgages they are twice as likely to go into foreclosure.*

If you're being quoted a subprime loan it's critical to shop around with at least two other lenders. You also need to ask what credit score you need in order to avoid a subprime rate.

> *Jackson knew that an older collection and his two high credit card balances were going to force him to pay subprime rates for a used vehicle. What he didn't know (and didn't ask) was that he just needed to increase his score by 15 points. That would have reduced his rate by 9% and saved him $3,700 interest! Paying an extra $200 on one of his credit cards would have gotten the balance below 50% of his limit. That alone would have boosted his score enough to get away from subprime. If you think that the finance manager should have given Jackson the heads up, you're being naive. His income was based on a percentage of the interest charges: the higher the rate, the larger the profit.*

Knowing your score will allow you to make an informed decision of whether you would be better off to:

Wait a few months or so, and take the steps to move up your credit score first. (See the credit score chapter)

Not do the financing when the total interest can often make your payment 50–75% higher.

Accept the subprime rate and do whatever it takes to increase the down payment (to finance a lower amount) and reduce the length of the loan which cuts down the total interest charges.

Your first place to get the latest range of interest rates for credit cards, vehicle financing, or mortgage loans should be a quick look at: www.bankrate.com . Once you have the average rates for whatever you're considering buying, you can figure out how bad (or fair) the offer is.

Finally, at www.myfico.com you are able to see which credit scores will yield various interest rates.

For mortgage loans or refinancing, go to: achieve my goals – mortgages – find offer.

For vehicle loans, go to: achieve my goals – auto loans – best rates – more info.

Raise your expectations

Low expectations create even lower results. You will never exceed your own expectations. In any sport, if your attitude is just hoping you'll finish the game, the odds aren't good that you'll accomplish much more than that. When it comes to any financing, you need to get out of the mindset that you're lucky they will finance you. Change that stinkin' thinking around so that you believe instead, they are lucky to get your business!

You'd be surprised by how many people subconsciously just don't think they deserve any better. They have resigned themselves to their fate of this or that fee, or getting charged subprime interest rates once again, and have simply stopped fighting for anything better.

Are you feeling like a valued customer, being treated with respect, not taken for granted, given options and choices, and being educated and not just pressured? No matter what you are financing, that person or company is not the only one in the country.

For any financing, there are literally thousands of people and companies in the same business. Raise your standards and find one that respects you, and wants to earn your business.

Don't make credit a substitute for income

If you're currently in a lower than average income job, or don't have much money saved, it becomes critical for you to avoid borrowing money for any reason. Borrowing money or owing money will 100% of the time make your financial situation worse and not better! Any borrowing puts you into a vicious cycle: smaller (or no) savings tends to mean more borrowing, at higher rip-off rates, which results in more interest paid out of a smaller average income. Your below-average income now drops even more because you'll need to make monthly payments, which makes it nearly impossible to save anything at all, and can have you at a payday lender to pay last month's bills with more borrowed money.

Not being able to borrow because of your current debt load, a lack of income, or a decent credit score can also be a blessing. After all, you can't get ripped off on your financing if you're paying cash. Plus you won't have payments that you knew all along would be hard to make, and would totally kill your budget and available cash each month.

Even if you can borrow – it doesn't mean you should. Sometimes what you can't do or can't have actually turns out to be a blessing: 100% of renters didn't get scammed by crooked mortgage brokers in the last housing bubble. Not a single renter in the country got caught in a foreclosure, and 100% of people who drove a paid-for used car didn't get repossessed if they lost their job.

Dealing With a Collection Agency

*About 30 million Americans have an average of
$1,500 of debt that is subject to collection.*
Consumer Financial Protection Bureau

Collectors deal with more than a hundred files each and every day. It is psychological warfare and many collectors (some would say most) aren't that interested in following the law. They want to trigger an emotional response in you and will press whatever button it takes to get you to pay them. Whether you legitimately owe the money or not, is often secondary. Whether the debt is way over the legal time they can collect from you, it isn't a big deal if you don't know your rights. And putting the heat on one of your aging parents because they can't get in touch with you directly is just the means to an end.

They will do whatever it takes: threats, lies, intimidation, buddy-buddy, appealing to your morals, anger, frustration, anxiety, having you freak out whenever the phone rings. They'll make you wonder if they really can send you to jail, making you believe that not paying will cost you your job, making you worry that the next knock at the door is the sheriff… they will do whatever it takes to make you pay them. Yes, there are collectors who have morals and will stay within the law. Unfortunately, they are certainly not in the majority, and they will either leave the business or change to scare-tactics sooner, rather than later.

There's a direct connection to how badly a collector can get under your skin and how likely you are to do whatever it takes to make the stress and phone calls stop. It isn't right, it's not legal, but you and 99% of everyone they contact don't know their rights and that's what collectors count on in order to be successful.

Tens of millions of people each year are exposed to the legal and illegal tactics of collection agencies for one write-off, medical bill, credit card debt, or another. Even today, upwards of three million people are getting harassed by collection agencies for late charges, or supposedly non-returned movies, from the long defunct Hollywood Video (or Movie Gallery in some states). One collection agency simply reported collections on half a million people's credit files and then waited for these people to find out that these collections prevented them from borrowing, or had plummeted their credit score. As these people then called the agency, the agency would update the collection, or remove it, for payment of the supposed past-due amount, plus a $75 fee. Their tactics continue to this day, but at least in this matter, a 2011 court order to settle one class action lawsuit now prevents collection agencies from reporting these items to the credit bureau.

With a mindset of doing *whatever it takes*, collection agencies frequently report an item on your credit file in order to blackmail you into paying it.

You may not be able to get blood from a stone, but collectors don't actually believe that saying.

Common collection agency tricks and lies

An entire list of the tricks and deceptive practices from collectors could fill its own book. Here are five of the more common ones, and how to deal with them:

We have proof that you owe this debt. Under federal law, collection agencies have to prove that you actually owe the money. A dispute letter is your critical step to giving them notice of that. By law, collection agencies have to mail you something called a five-day letter after first contact. This letter will outline the amount owed and the name of the original creditor on whose behalf they are collecting. The letter will also include a section of how to dispute the debt under the Fair Debt Collection Act. Remind the collector of this requirement under the law.

During this first call, insist they send the original contract to you (supposedly) signed, the credit card application they claim you signed, or whatever original documentation they are relying upon to prove it is your debt. They won't do it. You'll likely get a lot of 'we don't have to do that' or 'you should remember', or other evasive answers. The majority of third-party collection agencies have nothing but the amount, your name, and some contact information. When you do receive this five-day letter, it starts the clock for a 30-day period within which you have to write them and formally demand documentation and proof of the debt. They, in turn, must comply within five days.

> *Hurray for Maryland! In 2012 the state passed legislation that now forces collection agencies suing someone to provide proper proof of the debt, that it's the actual person they're suing, and that the debt is within the state's Statute of Limitation. If you don't live in Maryland, your state legislators could pass a similar law within a day, if they cared enough to want to do it...*

There is no Statute of Limitation on this. That's never true. Every debt has a legal time limit. Beyond that, collectors can still attempt to collect, but have no legal recourse against you and are prohibited from putting the matter on your credit report. This so-called Statute of Limitation is different for each state. You have to know if the debt is still within the time limit to pursue the matter against you. The other lie they may tell you is that the Statute of Limitation applies to credit reporting, but not to the collection of the debt.

The Credit Info Center has an excellent chart by state and even quotes you the statute number at:

www.creditinfocenter.com – then go to: credit repair – Statute of Limitation on debt.

For example, in Kansas, the Statute of Limitation for a credit card debt is three years as per State statute 60-512. With that, and a written letter sent by certified mail (return receipt requested) to the collection agency, you should be well on your way to being done with the matter.

Making a verbal settlement. If you reach a settlement on a debt, you must get it in writing. Verbal agreements are meaningless and cannot be enforced. It will be your word against theirs, and your next wave of collection calls will be with a different person three cubicles over. If it's not in writing and sent to you via fax, mail, or email with their company name on it, it isn't true and didn't happen! Of course, collectors will do whatever they can to avoid committing themselves in writing. If they won't put it in writing, tell them to re-contact you when they have changed their mind and want the money – period. It may be days or weeks but when they want your money, they *will* put it in writing.

You have to pay by credit card or bank account debit. Collectors will insist that you can only pay by credit card or by giving them your bank account information. Never ever do it. What you would be doing is just giving them a down-payment. They will, more times than not, take a much larger amount out of your bank account or from your credit card. Even with a settlement letter, you will now be fighting for months (probably unsuccessfully) to get back the overpayment. The only way you ever pay a collection agency is to mail a bank draft or money order. It will be for a fixed amount, and not the equivalent of giving them a blank check.

Just pay us something today. The most basic collection efforts are to get you to pay them something, even if it's just $10, just to show you're serious. While that may seem reasonable, if you do owe the debt, this simple request is designed to trap you. Firstly, the debt may be past the Statute of Limitation in your state. Even just a few dollars paid towards it can re-activate the debt, and can re-set the clock on its legal validity for another three to five years. The second trap is that any 'today' payment, no matter how small, would be by credit card, or by giving them your bank information. As explained above, the odds that the collector will take only the agreed to $10, is very tiny. Since you cannot prove any of your verbal agreements in court, you will be out the full balance, or whatever they can grab if you allow them access to your accounts.

Another critical point is that you must retain a copy of your settlement letter and bank draft receipt as proof. If not, you may well be going through this nightmare again. Every person who has to settle and pay a collection a second time is paying a heavy price for not keeping one piece of paper proving it's already been paid. Collection agencies 'forget' that you have paid the matter, they may 'forget' to take the matter off your credit file, or report it as paid in full. You'll need the proof to remind them, or to dispute the matter with the credit bureaus. As often as collection agencies purchase a large block of written-off debts, the can also re-sell them. If your file is re-sold, or not shown as paid in full, you will get a new collection agency calling you – often years later.

Fishing expedition collections

Just like many of the Hollywood Video accounts, millions of collections originate when the agencies bulk purchase thousands of written-off accounts. They may be from a credit card company, magazine issuer, fitness club, or other sources. At most, collection agencies pay three to 10 cents on the dollar for the outstanding balances. But, as you can imagine, they receive very little information with the accounts.

In these cases, their shotgun approach is to contact every possible person with the same or similar name. Their collection tactics won't be any different, even if you keep disputing on the phone that it's not you. These rogue collections average getting around 13% of the amounts owed, but often from someone who just wants them to stop calling – even if they pay something they've never owed. When the collection matter clearly isn't yours, no matter how small the amount, don't give in or give up by paying the balance. As with other collections, follow the steps of insisting on your five-day letter and dispute the item in writing.

How to settle a collection

In an ideal world you'd have the money to settle a debt which is legally owed, for 10 cents on the dollar, and have the collection removed from your credit bureau. Unfortunately, that isn't likely to happen. There is no black or white answer of how much of a settlement you can expect to negotiate. Do remember that the account has likely added a ton of interest and various fees and late charges. So the first question (of your research) should be to get the original amount you owed. Offering that as a settlement may already be 50 cents on the dollar or less.

In general, the older the debt, the longer it's been since the last payment, the lower the odds they believe they will ever get paid. That makes the discount higher for older debts, and even more so for items which are beyond the legal Statute of Limitation.

You may wish to pay them, but they cannot legally sue you for the debt.

What you do need to assure is that you only offer a settlement when you actually have the money set aside to pay them. You can settle a debt for six or 12 payments, but generally, collection agencies would rather have a little less money today than a little more down the road. If the settlement is by payments, you always need to mail each money order, and never use post dated checks or they'll have your banking information.

The main reason you'll want to pay the collection in full is to start the healing of your credit score. The impact of this collection is significant for the first three years. If you pay it in full and it's reported to the credit bureaus, the three-year countdown starts immediately. If you make payments over two years, it'll keep reporting as an outstanding collection. In that case, it'll be two years of payments and then the three years of healing. In that case, it's a total of five years before the major negative impact on your score starts to diminish.

Remember that these third-party collection agencies likely paid less than 10 cents on the dollar and would love to get paid something, sometime soon. No, they won't take your first low offer. They may even claim it can't be settled for anything less than the full amount. In that case, give them your offer and tell them to call you back when they want the money. Then hang up the phone and send a short letter offering the settlement in writing. In the letter (and in all of your conversations with the collector) you need to tell them:

You will settle the debt for this specific amount.

You will pay them by money order immediately after they send a written confirmation of the settlement showing:

The account number and original creditor's name on whose behalf they are collecting.

This one-time payment will be settlement in full.

They confirm removal (if you can negotiate this) or update your three credit bureau files to show payment in full.

The process may take a month or more, and a number of back and forth calls. Do stay persistent, stand your ground, and don't give in. It's also helpful to call them every few weeks as you will get a different person with every call and may get someone who will agree to your terms. Make one of the calls near the end of the month. Just like car dealers will make you a better deal on the 29th than the 5th, collectors also have goals and bonus plans they want to reach. Your settlement offer is more attractive if you can guarantee to get the money order into their hands by the end of the month.

*Always keep your conversations to two minutes or less.
Stick to the facts, don't get emotional, and don't look
for any sympathy or understanding. It would be
like waiting at a bus stop for an airplane...*

If you get sued

The National Consumer Law Center reports that about a million people are sued each year by collectors. Don't confuse being sued by collectors that the collectors actually know whether these people owe the money, whether they're within the Statute of Limitation, or whether they even have the right to sue. They do and they will. What happens once they file the lawsuit is entirely up to you.

Collection agencies do have the right to sue you for a debt they believe you owe. Until then, you may get letters from seemingly important law firms, which are actually just their in-house collectors. These letters are part of a series of steps designed to intimidate you. However, once you get served with court papers, you really are being sued. It's something you can never ever ignore. Whether you're broke and unemployed, or have the money, you must make the time to attend in court.

When you show up on the court date, you are simply there asking them to prove that you owe the debt (show me the documents I signed) and that it's legal for them to still collect (within your state's Statute of Limitation). If you don't show up, just like your favorite football team will forfeit the game, you automatically lose. It's the biggest thing collection agencies wish for, and it happens most of the time. Not showing up immediately enters a default judgment against you. If you're not there, the collection agency never needs to supply any proof that the lawsuit is legitimate at all. The courts go on the assumption that, if you're not there, you're admitting to owing it – period.

If you get sued you must show up in court. It's either show up or pay up. Not showing up in court turns a phony collection, with no legal way of collecting, into an air-tight judgment against you that they will now collect sooner rather than later.

You don't need an attorney for your court date. In fact, judges prefer to deal with you personally. You don't need to be Perry Mason, either. Just showing up puts you into the 10% of people who do, and may have the collection agency withdraw the matter or settle with you before the court appearance. If they do proceed, you just want a few questions answered:

Show me written proof that this is my debt.

Supply the breakdown of how the original amount got up to the current balance.

Document the date of this debt (and come prepared with the maximum time your state permits under the Statute of Limitation).

You'd be amazed at the huge percentage of files where the collection agency cannot answer those three basic questions. If they can't, the judge will dismiss the action and you're done with it, forever. The only thing left will be to force the collection agency to remove the action from your credit file. If they do have the backup documentation, explain to the judge that you have offered to settle the matter (if you have), and supply the dates of your calls and copies of your letters. The judge can often be a great help in getting the collection agency rep to accept a settlement right then and there. While collectors don't listen to you, they will always listen to a judge.

Medical collections: They'll really hurt you

It is estimated that upwards of $1 billion is collected each year by doctors, hospitals, and collection agencies which are not legally owed!

Over 30 million Americans have some kind of medical collection on their credit reports. The sick reality is that the majority of these are small amounts of $10, $20, or perhaps $100 at most. What's even more infuriating is that most of these people do have medical coverage and thought they had fully paid their balances or co-pay amounts. Suddenly, and often without notice, these small amounts from third parties involved in treatments such as tests and lab work, show up on a credit report.

These companies often have nothing more than a name and address, and without all the information they can't bill properly which is why they end up classifying them as collections.

The healthcare industry is the biggest client of collection agencies and makes up 42% of the collection business. With about $40 billion a year in unpaid hospital bills, collection agencies will never run out of business. But their tactics can also go too far – way too far. In Minnesota, the Attorney General is now pursuing collection agencies making their first collections right at someone's hospital bed. In fact, all over the country, over 60 collections agencies actually have offices right in hospitals. Nobody has yet decided if that breaks any laws; however, it's so wrong, and so sick, no matter what. The Attorney General called it aggressive and abusive, and that's putting it mildly.

Understanding your rights

Collection agencies collect around $40 billion a year.
About one in five calls to the FTC are complaints
about their practices. It is by far the number
one industry for complaints to the FTC.

If your finances have reached the point where collectors are calling you, it's imperative that you know your rights. The Fair Debt Collection Practices Act governs the behaviors, rights, and guidelines of the collection industry. You need to be informed, or you may well make a whole lot of bad decisions.

Collectors can contact friends and relatives to locate you, but they can't discuss the reasons, or share your financial information. Bank collectors have special exemptions under the law. They're actually able to tell neighbors, friends, or your employer where they are calling from and that they need to speak to you on an urgent matter. It may sound insane that they're exempt from the law, but that is what huge campaign contributions and lobbyists can achieve. Even when the financial institution can reach you directly, they will still call family members or your work. It's a pure intimidation and pressure tactic.

Collectors cannot harass or abuse you. However, just because they can't – doesn't mean they won't. At that point, you need to fight back. You have the right to have them stop contacting you. You'll need to do so in writing, and the links to standard form letters are listed below. As with all your contacts with a collector, do it in writing and send it certified mail, return receipt requested, to assure you always have a copy as proof. If it isn't in writing – it didn't happen! If you believe a collector has crossed the line, your first action should be to file a complaint with the Consumer Financial Protection Bureau which has now taken over the supervision of collection agencies. (The link and their web site is listed below.) Also send a copy of your complaint to the collection agency to put them on notice that you are serious in fighting back and protecting your rights. When all else fails, the Supreme Court has ruled that you do have the right to sue collection agencies for their breaches of federal law. While you may not want to go that far, it may be worth the money to have an attorney send a letter to remind them of their breach of the law and your rights. Collection agencies are in the business of collecting money and not paying it out by getting sued.

Get informed and fight back

The Fair Debt Collection Practices Act from the Federal Trade Commission and extensive resources and information are at: www.usa.gov and search for "Fair Debt Collection Act".

Watch a short video of your rights with debt collectors from the Federal Trade Commission at: www.consumer.ftc.gov –then go to: video & media.

Sample letters to use when contacting collection agencies and a consumer friendly guide to explaining your rights at: www.privacyrights.org – then go to: debt collection.

To file a complaint with the Consumer Financial Protection Bureau: www.consumerfinance.gov.

File the same complaint with your state's Attorney General office through the link of the National Association of Attorneys General: www.naag.org.

To file a complaint with the Federal Trade Commission: www.ftc.gov – then go to: consumer protection – file a complaint.

Mortgages: Please Don't Owe Until Death Do You Part

There are really only two ways to buy a house – with your money or with someone else's money. What would baby boomers of past generations have done without the huge equity they accumulated in their principal residences? They achieved this equity through hard beginnings, a pretty tight budget, a down payment, and a mortgage.

Every year, millions of Americans deal with a mortgage in one way or another. Many will reach their dreams of becoming first-time homeowners with the help of a mortgage. Others may buy bigger homes, and some may refinance their current loans. In today's market, where prices haven't recovered from their peak of just a few years ago, millions of families are now able to afford a home.

But for each buyer today, there are four million unique stories of families who lost their homes due to foreclosures. From the peak of house prices in 2006, to the bottom in 2011, more than five trillion dollars of equity was wiped out. Hardest hit were families who purchased a home in the years prior to the peak and especially those with only a small or no down payment.

True, nobody forced these families to buy a home at that exact time, and nobody made them take out some very questionable loans. However, just as they decided to assume a lot of responsibility, these families got a lot of 'help' from banks, brokers, Wall Street, rating agencies, mortgage servicers, and many others. Families placed their trust in the system and in the regulators. They trusted that the largest banks in the country would do the right things, and that mortgage brokers would counsel them on options and risks, just as much as they did on rates and payments. None of that happened.

> *"Let's hope we're all wealthy and retired*
> *before this house of cards collapses."*
> Internal email at one of the rating agencies
> released by the Justice Department

Lower income families were sold on the idea that it wouldn't be hard at all for them to own a home. People with minimal income were 'helped' with a NINJA loan that stood for: no income, no job, no assets. Some lenders rented entire hotel ballrooms to process loans by the thousands, creatively filling in blanks on loan documents and forging signatures on others. At the height of the housing bubble, half of all subprime loans were liar loans totalling more than $300 billion. It didn't take long after that to trigger the worst recession in 70 years with massive ripple effects throughout the global economy.

All these years later, an eternity in the world of finance and lending, regulators have finally caught up to some of the questionable or fraudulent practices. Vast numbers of banks and lenders have written settlement checks for billions of dollars. Of course, it was all done without admitting any liability… after all, that's the purpose of a settlement… here's some money, now go away and leave us alone…

> *In pro sports, the penalties are suspensions: No play – no pay. If the law allowed regulators to suspend the licenses of banks and mortgage brokers from conducting any mortgage lending for three or six months, they'd feel the pain and would never repeat their behaviors. It would need to be done just once to one lender. Right now, billions of dollars of fines on tens of billions of dollars of income have the equivalent financial impact of you getting a speeding ticket.*

Also caught up in the waves upon waves of foreclosures were vast numbers of families who shouldn't have been foreclosed on at all! Yes, families lost their homes due to the actions of banks and mortgage servicers (often departments within the banks). In early 2013, banks paid an estimated $8.5 billion in settlements in what regulators described as repeated and pervasive breaches of the law. So far, nobody has gone to jail and it's not entirely clear that many lessons were learned, or that new regulations are now tight enough to prevent another massive meltdown.

Shopping for a mortgage loan

In the new reality following the financial meltdown, the Consumer Financial Protection Bureau (CFPB) implemented a large range of new regulations. In short, lenders must verify your income and other debts and ensure that you can afford your payments. The CFPB calls these qualified mortgage standards and, if followed, will protect lenders from liabilities down the road. That pretty much assures you that lenders will follow these guidelines. As a result, you'll need to be ready to supply at least two recent pay stubs and last year's tax return. There may be more, but that will depend on the lender you choose.

Many of these new requirements are just common sense. It's that common sense, along with morals and compassion that left the lending industry for about a decade. If these requirements seem inconvenient, they really aren't. Think of it as a level playing field where everyone supplies the same information, where an approval actually means something, and where not everyone who can sign their name can get a $200,000 loan. When you're approved and have your new home, it'll also be a blessing that these common sense requirements and regulations should prevent another housing meltdown in the foreseeable future.

Shopping for a mortgage loan has nothing to do with convenience, and where you currently bank is irrelevant. It's not as if you're ever going to visit your mortgage company for coffee. It's all about the rate, fees, and terms with a credible lender who is giving you a pre-approval. An actual pre-approval, along with a commitment letter, will outline your down payment and set the maximum you qualify for. It will also lock-in your interest rate for up to three months before the loan has to be in place.

With new lending rules, your maximum total debts cannot exceed 43% of your gross income. Prior to these new guidelines, the most that could go towards your mortgage loan (the front end ratio) was 28%, and your total payment obligations (back end ratio) couldn't exceed 36%. The maximum 43% includes your new mortgage loan payment, plus payments on whatever else you owe. That's everything from the minimum payment on your credit cards, your vehicle and student loans, and any other payments. However, just because a lender's math says you can afford it, doesn't mean you actually can. Being broke is no fun at all. It's a huge amount of stress just to keep your head above water. You need to do the math up front to honestly decide if you can afford what you're taking on. After the fact, your payments won't magically change, self-adjust, or reduce and your reality of living in your dream home will quickly turn into a nightmare. Things can go wrong, incomes can drop, layoffs can happen, and credit cards can get maxed.

How much are you currently saving? That, plus what you're currently paying for housing costs is the most you can afford. That's assuming you're willing to live without a single dollar of cushion each month and must also include insurance, extra utilities, mortgage insurance, and taxes.

With a 43% maximum debt ratio you can calculate what payments you can afford before visiting your lender. For example:

Total gross monthly income:	$4,000
43% maximum total debt payments can be:	$1,720
(gross income x 43%)	
Deduct all your current minimum payments:	
Minimum credit card payment:	$120
Student loan payment:	$210
Vehicle payment:	$322
Which leaves as maximum available:	$1,068

(this is your maximum total debt payment minus your current payments)

Knowing that the math says you can have a maximum of $1,068 for your new mortgage payment, now just find any online calculator to see what price of home, minus your down payment, you can afford. Of course, you'll also need to make the critical decision of how long of a mortgage term you'll choose.

If you need help or more information, there are many sites online. One of the better ones is from the Department of Housing and Urban Development (HUD). Their information ranges from buying a home to avoiding a foreclosure. They also discuss your rights, and the obligations of your lender and mortgage servicer at: www.hud.gov – then go to: buy a home.

One good resource site (amongst many) that includes mortgage calculators, what-if scenarios on pre-payments, one-time extra payments, or getting a full amortization schedule is at: www.hsh.com.

Common mortgage jargon

Conventional and conforming loans

Conventional loans are all those loans which are not VA, FHA, or USDA loans, which are described in the next section. They're offered by everybody from credit unions to banks to various other financial institutions. In short, if you don't have a VA or FHA loan, you have a conventional (call it 'normal') loan.

The second criterion is determined by whether or not your loan is conforming. In other words, does it fall within the guidelines and limits of Fannie Mae and Freddie Mac? These two giants control most of the mortgage business in the country by providing a secondary market. They purchase mortgages from lenders, hold some, but re-sell most of them as investments. In fact, Fannie Mae (Federal National Mortgage Association) is the largest source of residential mortgage funds in the country, having funded the loans of more than 55 million households since 1968. Freddie Mac (Federal Home Loan Mortgage Corporation) has financed over 7 million single-family homes over the past four years.

Both of these conglomerates are stockholder-owned corporations which are chartered by Congress. They sell their loan portfolios in large blocks to investors. That's the reason for their specific standards and requirements. The fact that both got stuck with billions of dollars of loans, which turned out to be risky during the run-up to the housing meltdown, is another matter. But many of the large banks have also paid billions of fines for sticking Fannie Mae and Freddie Mac with loans that really shouldn't have been made and certainly didn't conform.

When a loan exceeds its maximum amount, it is referred to as a nonconforming, or a jumbo loan. Jumbo loans are offered at slightly higher rates and can also have some additional requirements. The actual limits which make your loan conforming can change each year. The current conforming loan limit for first mortgages is $417,000 for single-family homes. They're 50% higher in Alaska, Guam, Hawaii, and the Virgin Islands, and high-cost areas will have a maximum of $625,000. Second mortgages also have limits, but the total loan value of the first and second mortgages cannot exceed this total.

FHA and VA mortgages

The Federal Housing Administration (FHA) was established in order to assist lower to middle income Americans to purchase a home. It allows families in these groups access to federal insurance against losses for lenders who make their mortgages within specific rules and guidelines.

The Department of Veterans Affairs (VA) assists veterans and active duty personnel in purchasing their principal residence. Together, the FHA and VA, as well as the Farmers Home Administration, handle around one-fifth of residential mortgages in the country. For both of these programs, the standard debt and mortgage payment ratios can be a little more lenient.

Subprime rates

A subprime mortgage is one that's made to anyone with a lower credit score that does not qualify for a conventional loan. A lower credit score is equated with a higher risk and thus a higher rate – a much higher rate. These types of mortgage loans started the housing meltdown, and they certainly haven't gone away.

The credit score cut-off, that may force you to look at a subprime loan, can change and will vary between lenders. That makes it even more critical to know your credit score and check a few online mortgage sites that will show you the current score required to obtain a conventional mortgage. Never ever accept the first answer or the first offer. Over a decade of studies have shown that up to half of all subprime borrowers could have qualified for conventional loans. In fact, during congressional hearings, one of the major subprime lenders disclosed some shocking internal information. They stated that more than 19% of their clients actually had a credit score of 660 or higher. That is a figure which should never be charged subprime rates! Another 22% had scores of 620 to 660, which also should not have made subprime rates automatic at that time.

Subprime should never be your first or only option. If it is, it'll be very expensive. The average subprime borrower obtaining a mortgage through a broker pays $5,200 more than obtaining the loan directly from a lender, according to an extensive study by the Center for Responsible Lending.

If your credit score is close to qualifying for a conventional loan, it always pays to wait. Collections get older and have less impact on your credit score, and paying down some balances can quickly increase your score as well. If you've applied for a loan and have consistently received only a subprime approval, you can also ask what to do. Lenders do want your business and the reputable ones (that aren't excited and pushy about jamming you into a subprime loan to make huge profits) will give you some feedback as to what you need to do to change it. Asking the questions and having the patience to wait will save you tens of thousands of dollars of interest. It'll also avoid you from having a payment you will barely be able to afford.

HELOC

This acronym is short for a Home Equity Line of Credit (HELOC). For renovations, a consolidation, or other reasons, many people believe this is their best financial alternative. Since a HELOC is over and above your mortgage loan, it requires a fair amount of equity to be able to set it up. That's a problem when your home's value isn't high enough to give you the equity to borrow against.

While they can seem like a good idea at the time, a HELOC is still a mortgage. It's still pledging your house for collateral and risking your home for whatever you're using the credit line for. The interest rate is adjustable, so when rates start to go up, your payment and interest can and will increase the following month. If your ultimate goal is to be mortgage free, any line of credit which requires interest-only payments will never be paid off. It'll take a lot of discipline for you to regularly and consistently make higher payments so some money does go to pay down the balance.

> *A caller recently shared that she and her husband were two months away from paying off their mortgage. As I was heading for the fridge to pull out some champagne, she volunteered that they also had a $100,000 HELOC. Stop! What? OK, let's not kid each other here. That means they're a long way from a mortgage burning party. The line of credit is secured against their home – and it counts! It's kind of like saying we're debt free except for that $18,000 credit card. Nice try...*

As to how the HELOC got to have a balance of close to $100,000, the caller was more evasive. "Well, it was a little of helping the kids and a new this and that"... and, "you know how it is." No, I don't. But isn't that so true? A few thousand here and there doesn't seem like much at the time. And it's so easy because they can just write a check and pay interest only. But looking in the rear-view mirror, it's a huge amount and will certainly delay their original retirement plans.

If you have a HELOC, what are the major items that make up your balance? If you're like many people, you may not immediately remember. Perhaps you used it to pay off some credit cards? That seemed like a logical way to reduce your rates, but what are your credit card balances right now? If you have balances on the cards again, the balance transfer was a mistake. If you've run the cards up again and haven't paid off the old balance, you've only moved the debt around. Now you owe double what you did before the change-over. Are you paying way more than just interest-only on your HELOC? If not, you've now stretched the payback of your old credit card balances out to a decade or two. You could have had high credit card rates and focused for a year or two on paying them off and been done with them. Instead, you have a lower rate, but for a significantly longer period of time making the interest more in total, and not saving you money.

Think back not that many years ago. You used to get a loan if you wanted to borrow $10,000 for renovations or $15,000 for a motorcycle. Well, making a loan costs the bank about $200 to $300 in setups, credit reports, etc. So they started to convert these loans to lines of credit. A loan has a three, four, or five-year term of fixed payments. Make all the payments and you are done with this debt. A credit line now makes you the loan officer. You can pay as

little as interest-only (newsflash: most do), or as much as
you want. You were sold on convenience, flexibility, and
the continuous availability of credit. All three, however are
a total win-lose: a win for the bank and trouble for you.

On average, it now takes more than a decade to pay off a line
of credit – if ever. That's assuming you don't just roll it into
a mortgage refinance. It used to be four years of loan interest,
now it's a decade or more. This is great for lenders – very
bad for you. With all other payments, it's just natural to fall
back on the least amount you can pay – and you do. Banks
have the brightest marketing minds in the country. They're so
great at selling you something that's massively profitable for
them and in turn helps you with your going-broke plan.

Whether it's this time or next time, take out a home equity
loan instead. It will fix your interest rate and payments and you'll
know exactly when you're done. They typically come in terms of
five, 10, or 15-years. The five year rate will be great, 10-year is OK,
and 15-year rate is pretty high. If at all possible in your realistic
budget, always take the five year term.

With a home equity loan you will have some minimal closing
costs, so you will need to shop around for the rate and your total
costs. Generally, your best deal will be at your credit union. A home
equity line of credit, instead of a loan, will have lower payments, but
you'll likely owe the money two or three times longer.

What matters more:
Rate, balance, term or payment?

Would an extra four dollars a month change your financial
life in a big way? There was a recent radio campaign from one of
the major banks: Switch your credit line to us and save half a

percent in interest. Plus, the guy in the commercial says he now sleeps much better and worries less.

Yes, most ads are based on the premise that you're not that informed and assume you can't do math. If you don't owe anything on your credit line, the rate doesn't matter. If you owe $10,000, a half percent interest savings amounts to four dollars a month. That's going to help you sleep better and worry less? Even with a $20,000 balance, it's an eight dollar a month savings. The ad may sound great, but shouldn't get you excited.

Financial trouble happens when you focus solely on the rate or the payment. As the example in the HELOC section describes, they'll have some of the lowest rates and lowest payments. But you'll owe the money for a lifetime. When it comes to borrowing, there are four things you'll need to know:

The balance or total amount you're borrowing

The interest rate

The term of the loan – how long you'll owe the money

The payment per month

The payment is the least important factor. Of course it has to fit your budget, but you can pretty much have any payment you want – you just have to stretch the term. The rate matters more and more only if you owe a lot of money, *and* you owe it for a long period of time. You're better off owing $5,000 at 20% for a year ($1,000 interest) than owing $5,000 at 6% for a decade ($1,660 interest)! The faster you pay something off, the less your rate matters since the debt won't be around for long.

That leaves the balance, or the total amount you owe or borrow. That is the most important factor. If you don't borrow anything – the rate doesn't matter and your payment will be ZERO!

Want to guess how many foreclosures, collections, repossessions, or legal actions happen to people who don't owe money or don't finance what they buy? None!

If you can lower what you owe, borrow less, reduce your renovation budget, take some of your savings as a down payment, or do any one of a dozen debt-reducing tactics, those will matter. Focus on what you're paying and not what you're saving. Focus on the balance and the term more than the rate.

15 or 30-Year mortgage?

Own a home not a mortgage

Longer term or shorter is a question that has a different answer for different sets of needs, risk tolerances, budgets, and comfort levels. Nothing feels better than to have a long-term loan with a fixed rate when rates are increasing. But a longer term also comes with a higher interest rate as lenders are risking their returns (interest income) over a much longer period.

Perhaps for you, nothing feels better than to know that the end of your loan is actually within sight – sooner, rather than later. It's something that more and more people are choosing to strive for. Since 2007, the percentage of people opting for a 15-year fixed term has almost tripled. The payoff is huge if your goal is to be mortgage and debt-free, because the best mortgage is no mortgage at all.

Current pain = future gain
Current gain = future pain

Choosing a 15-year mortgage will certainly have a higher payment. It may also be more difficult to qualify for, since the higher payment does have to fit your debt ratio. Is it worth paying off your loan in half the time? Only you can decide – only you can set your financial goals and choose your debt freedom date.

Your decision doesn't need to be an 'either-or'. Twenty-year loans and other terms are becoming more common, and readily offered by most lenders. If possible, these loans will get you away from the forever plan, to something that may better fit your budget, save you huge amounts of interest, and save you a decade of payments. Five minutes on a web site with mortgage calculators will give you all the information and numbers you'll need to make an informed decision. One popular web site with more than 70 different calculators is at: www.bankrate.com – then go to: calculators.

Adjustable rate mortgages

Adjustable Rate Mortgages (ARMs), or hybrid adjustable mortgages, are available in a wide variety of terms ranging from 1, 3, 5, 7 or even 10 years. Because they are adjustable, they generally come with a lower starting interest rate and often include a convertible feature which allows them to be changed to a fixed rate term after a specific period. ARMs generally adjust their rate every six or twelve months after that point. There can also be extended periods of time when interest rates are stable and mortgage rates don't change much at all. If you know for certain that you will sell your home in a few years, an ARM may save on interest-costs over the shorter term, with minimal risks of getting caught with large rate increases.

These types of loans can come with very attractive rates. It was these so-called teaser rates that played a large part in creating the mortgage meltdown. As a result, always be mindful of buyer beware: they are introductory or teaser rates designed to do just that, lure you into taking the offer. As the words imply, these are interest rates that will be adjusted at some point. Nobody knows with any certainty how interest rates will move in the future. Experts can make predictions, but they are not making your payments, or gambling on your financial future.

The decision on whether to get a fixed rate or an ARM is one that only you can make. The difference between a 30-year fixed rate and an adjustable rate is usually around half a percent. Whatever your balance is, multiply it by 0.5% and divide by 12 to get the actual difference per month. That figure is what you'd pay for the security of knowing your payments are fixed and your rate will never ever jump. Conversely, that's the amount you could save if you choose to risk that rates will be the same or lower when your ARM adjusts. The decision is always yours. If the actions of others matter in your decision, Freddie Mac issues an annual refinance transition report. Of their customers in a one-year ARM, 82% refinanced to a fixed rate, and even two-thirds of customers with a longer term ARM moved to the safety of a fixed rate.

While an ARM is not a wise choice for the vast majority of people, at least some notice is available to you now: new regulations introduced in 2013 now requires mortgage servicers to notify you seven months in advance of any adjustments. Their letter needs to include an approximation of your new payments, the new estimated rate, and alternatives to renewing your ARM.

When Linda bought her home she certainly didn't have any plans of moving again. Her broker discussed getting a fixed or adjustable mortgage and talked her into a five year adjustable. From what Linda remembers, the payments would be approximately $55 less each month. She does clearly remember the broker stating that 'the rate changes are capped so it'll never really go up much...' The first increase was $85. It was a shock to Linda, but she justified *it in that she was only paying about $30 more a month now from the fixed rate she could have chosen. The second increase was $70 a month and had now increased her payments by $155. Her broker was wrong or had misled her, but Linda knew she couldn't live for a better past or go back in time to make the safe decision…*

Reverse mortgages

In the words of one financial commentator, reverse mortgages are a good idea if you hate your kids. While that's a pretty strong statement, it's also accurate. Reverse mortgages allow seniors to take the equity out of their principal residences without having to sell their properties, or make any further payments during the rest of their lifetimes towards their homes. It can be somewhere between the only option and the worst possible idea.

The amount of money that can be advanced with a reverse mortgage depends on your age and the appraisal of the property. Someone aged 62, for example, will receive a lot less money than someone aged 75. Since there won't be payments to make, and the lender cannot force you out of your home, and they will need to estimate how long they'll be holding this mortgage. If you're married, you also need to be aware of the fine print in your documents. If only one of you signs on the loan, in the event the signer passes away, the other loses the right to stay in the home. The balance is due and payable immediately or the lender will foreclose on the surviving partner.

If you do choose to sell at some point, or when you pass away, the lender will be repaid for all the money advanced and all accumulated interest. If any significant amount of time has passed, the lender essentially owns the house, because of the size of the outstanding balance. Fees alone can often approach 10% of the mortgage amount. While these huge fees have dropped in recent years due to lower demand, and as more people understand the implications of a reverse mortgage, it still makes a reverse mortgage a last resort, and not a first choice.

A reverse mortgage is a financial option, but it should always be your last option. Depending on your income, you may qualify for a small conventional mortgage through a credit union or local bank. Many will also advance a line of credit secured by your home or a reverse mortgage credit line. Both of these alternatives give you access to the funds you may need but will only charge interest as you draw out the money. They'll also have almost none of the fees, a lot less interest, and you haven't signed your home over to a lender. If you have children, it's also a great idea to have an honest conversation with them if you are in serious need of additional money. With a reverse mortgage, the home will revert to the lender and will not be inherited by your children. A different option, that may be a win-win for your children, is for them to make you an interest and payment-free loan and take a lien against your home. If you sell the home, or when you pass away, the sale of the home will allow repayment of the loan, and title will pass to your heirs.

Before you decide, there's a web site with vast amounts of practical and easy to understand information at: www.reverse.org.

Timeshares

Some people love their timeshare or the chance to trade for a different resort every year. If you're like most people, however, you love it only for the first few years and then you realize you're saddled with a forever annual maintenance fee that keeps increasing, one you cannot control or avoid.

With an average price of $18,000, timeshares lose almost all of their value the moment you sign the documents. They're not an investment but an obligation. You are renting a permanent holiday at a very high price and with a very high pressure sales pitch. That free weekend you were offered to check it out will cost you a huge amount of money and likely some significant regret in the future.

Timeshares have become like the lyrics from the Eagles song Hotel California: you can check out anytime you like, but you can never leave. If you own a timeshare, hopefully you enjoy it and use it each year, because the private resale market is almost non-existent. If you want proof, go to Ebay and you'll be able to confirm that rather quickly. Here are some recent timeshare listings for sale: Grand Cayman for $77, Maui for $199, Foxrun in North Carolina for $50, and Colorado at Copper Mountain for $2. It gets better if you think that $200 or even two dollars is too expensive. There are listings for a dollar in Cabo in Mexico, Oceanfront at Cocoa Beach Florida, Orlando, and at Whistler, British Columbia.

Even at a buck, people cannot give them away. Why? Because you will have a $600 to $1,200 annual maintenance fee forever. That's not even counting the tens of thousands of people who still owe money on their timeshares and thus can't even give them away without writing a check to first pay off the balance of their loan.

What happens when tens of thousands of desperate people want to unload something at all cost? The scams start up – and there are dozens. Anyone promising to help you to sell your timeshare requesting any amount of money up front is scamming you, and lying to you – period. Just google the phrase 'timeshare resale scam' and you'll see more than 140,000 horror stories, angles, pitches, and frauds. If you were defrauded already, the calls won't stop. The next call you may get is a new scam called a reload. This caller will share that they know you spent a lot of money but haven't received any help with your sale. They then claim that they are able to go after the previous company to get you a refund. And a second scam is born… for another fee… from the same scamsters.

If you have a timeshare, there are some legitimate resource sites, user groups, and perhaps ideas on selling your unit.

Donate for a Cause may take your timeshare for a tax receipt, if it qualifies. For most, you will need to pay between $1,000 and $2,000. Yes, it adds insult to financial injury, but it may be your only way to stop the financial bleeding of annual fees. They're at: www.donateforacause.org.

One of the largest timeshare user groups with indispensable information for every owner is at: www.tug2.net.

Mortgage insurance

With a down payment of less than 20%, lenders require your loan to be insured. With an even smaller amount of equity, private mortgage insurance (PMI) will protect you in case of default. Your benefit, by spending a large amount of money on insurance, is that it'll allow you to purchase a home with as little as a three to five percent down payment. However, just because you can do it, doesn't mean you should do it. For obvious reasons, as the past few years have shown, the smaller the down payment, the bigger your risk of being underwater, or being unable to sell your home.

The cost of insurance will vary between lenders and states. As with everything else, it'll pay to shop around. Your cost will also depend on your credit history and your down payment, since these are the two biggest risk factors for your lender. Insurers know that a large down payment will make you less likely to default, as will a higher credit score. The premiums are generally included in your loan payment, although you can choose to pay up front or annually. Costs are roughly $100 per $100,000 financed. The coverage insures the amount of your loan over 80%. For loans made under the Federal Housing Administration the coverage is generally more expensive since its coverage is for the entire loan amount.

To potentially avoid having to pay for PMI, many mortgage loans involve some sort of piggyback financing. These are alternative ways to structure your loan with less than a 20% down payment. If you have a 10% down payment, your loan can become an 80-10-10 loan. This avoids additional charges and fees, but it is always important for you to compare the cost of the second mortgage with the cost of mortgage insurance. Just avoiding some fees is pointless if the total interest on your second mortgage turns out to be more costly. After all, whether it is called a fee or interest, it's all money coming out of your pocket.

At some point, there will be an end to the PMI you're paying. Just as selling your car negates the need for car insurance, reaching 20% equity stops your mortgage insurance. It'll be up to you to prove that you now have sufficient equity. You'll need to know your mortgage balance and you will have to pay for an appraisal for your home. Call your PMI provider first if you believe that you have the equity to discontinue the premium. All companies have slightly different policies, as do Fannie Mae and Freddie Mac. You'll need to adhere to their rules and procedures or you may spend a lot of needless time, money, and energy.

Paying more – paying more often

According to the FDIC, less than 3% of people consistently
pay something extra on their mortgage loan

If your goal is to own your home outright, you are in a pretty elite group of only around 30% of the population, according to the U.S. Census Bureau. To accelerate reaching that day of mortgage freedom, there are a number of ways to accomplish your goal.

There aren't shortcuts to paying down your balance and there isn't any magic software program to do that for you – sorry. You'll need to pay a little more money each month, all of which will be applied directly to reducing your principal. The longer the term of your loan, the more it'll matter. Anytime you owe less the next month, the interest due will also be less.

If it's a challenge in your budget to pay some extra money with each loan payment, could you make a half payment each payday? One of the most effective ways of reducing your balance is to set up the payments on a bi-monthly basis. It simply takes your monthly payment, divides it by two, and has you paying half your monthly payment every two weeks. It can be relatively pain-free, because it's a much lower amount, matches your pay periods, and makes budgeting a lot easier. You're now making 26 half payments, which is the equivalent of 13 monthly payments. For example, if you payments are $800 a month, that's $9,600 a year. If you pay half of your $800 every two weeks, it's $400 paid 26 times a year, or $10,400.

You should contact your lender or mortgage servicer to confirm in writing (an email will normally suffice) that they can and will do this, and request the procedures you will need to follow. Don't fall for the pitch that you need to pay a fee around

$200 to $400. You'll pay and not gain. They may take the additional money from you each month, but will often deposit it to their account and only apply the additional money once a year, which won't gain you the regular principal reductions.

If making payments on a bi-monthly basis doesn't sound too tough – wonderful! Because it may not seem like a lot of money, but it'll quickly add up to tens of thousands of dollars in savings. Increasing the frequency or the amount of your payments are the only two ways to reduce your interest and pay down your balance quickly. There is no trick, no gimmick, no catch – just more money going towards the principal more often, which means less interest. It really is that simple.

Make sure you understand the difference in pre-paying your payments or pre-paying the principal. When you are pre-paying your payments, the lender will use this money against future monthly payments. So if you've sent some extra money, it can be used to pay next month's payment. Unless you tell your lender differently, it is the default way lenders treat extra money you send. When you want to pre-pay the principal, the extra money is applied directly to the balance. It will still take a payment the following month, but the principal reduction has reduced the interest from that point on, because you now owe a lesser amount of money. If that is your intent, make sure it is clearly marked on your check and the payment coupon.

> Mike had sent an extra $10,000 to be applied to his mortgage loan. Five years later, he was celebrating becoming debt free with his last payment. At that point, his lender advised him that he still had a balance of over $8,200! With some digging, it turned out that the money had been held towards pre-payments and was never applied to the principal! What Mike still owed was interest on this $10,000 for five years!

One common question or objection which really matters: "but I want to keep my tax deductible interest!" It's a bad idea and it's really bad math. While your mortgage likely has the lowest interest rate, it makes sense to first pay off all your consumer debt. But even at the lowest rate, the interest on your mortgage will add up to a lot more than you'll ever pay on any other borrowing.

If your income tax rate is 25% you'll likely get a tax refund on some of your loan interest. For example, if you pay $8,000 a year in interest, your 25% tax rate will get you a $2,000 refund. Great news: if you pay off your mortgage, you will no longer get the $2,000 deduction. Why is that great news? You're spending $8,000 interest a year and getting $2,000 back. The bottom line is that you're still out $6,000! If you're debt free you no longer have any loan payments and you're no longer spending that money. Don't let anyone tell you to keep your mortgage because of a tax deduction. They're telling you it's a great idea to spend $8,000 so you can get back a quarter of it and stay in debt forever.

Refinancing your loan

When it matters the most – most people don't.
Less than 50% of people shop around for a refi.

The world of refinancing has certainly changed drastically since the housing meltdown. With tighter lending rules, less equity, and much more conservative appraisals (to put it mildly), it's a much different world than just a few years ago. The good news is that re-financing legislation now gives you three days to back out if the lender is changing the terms of what was originally quoted. Lenders are no longer able to trap you at closing with the previous common bait and switch tactics of changing the rate, fees, or closing costs.

At the height of the housing market in 2006, over 90% of refi's were cash-outs for an average of $30,000. That translated to pulling $750 billion out of home equities, according to the Federal Reserve. It makes it a fair question to ask whether many of those families who got into financial trouble would have avoided it had they not increased their loan debt thereby increasing their balances. Today, according to Freddie Mac reports, only 19% of homeowners who refinance increase their loan by five percent or more. On the other hand, more than 35% lowered their loan amounts. In other words, because of low appraisals, more than one-third of refi's are actually cash-in. If you don't have sufficient equity because of your home value, a cash-in means you are adding a down-payment at closing to reduce your outstanding balance to now let you do the refi.

As a rough rule of thumb, if you're able to reduce your interest rate by one percent or more, a refi tends to make sense. You'll need to check the numbers, but that kind of interest reduction may save you a significant amount of interest. You'll need to assure that you do your homework first, and that should include some basic steps:

- Get at least three quotes: one from your current lender, one online, and one from a credit union.

- Your closing costs can't be more than your savings. As a rule of thumb, it shouldn't take longer than 24–30 months to cover your closing costs out of the payment savings.

- If you're close to being below the magic 80% financed amount, do whatever it takes to avoid having to pay mortgage insurance. Can you add some savings to reduce your balance in order to get to 20% equity?

- What kind of term will you take for your refi? That's actually the most critical decision you'll make. A refi can cost you a ton of extra money, or save you years of payments – it's up to you. The average refi in today's new reality comes after 4.6 years. In other words, the typical person has paid almost five years before refinancing. If that's you, what do you actually want to accomplish with a refi? Yes, it'll be a lower interest rate, but what's your goal? To reduce the payments, or the total you'll pay back? Will you go right back to a new 30-year term, or do what it takes to cut your loan down to 20 years? Your financial situation may not give you a choice, but if you do have an option, what matters to you? Short term thinking (loving the slightly lower payments…) will cost you dearly over the long run.

In a recent survey 52% of people aged 55–65 stated that they know they will have a mortgage payment in retirement. Your mortgage loan is your biggest monthly expense by far. How long do you want it around? What would your financial life be like if you were payment free?

Five minutes of math with any online calculator will give you all the numbers and motivation you need and the decision you make might be very different. For example, on a $150,000 loan balance with 25 years left, the payments are $880 a month, and you've already paid $53,000. Your refinance options are to:

- Take a new 30-year term at a one percent lower rate: $716 now, which is a $164 lower payment, but stretches the term another five years. Total payments: $257,800 (360 months x $716).

- Reduce the term to 20 years at a one percent lower rate: $908 now, which increases the payment by $28, but decreases the length of your payments by five years. Total payments: $218,000 (240 months x $908 per month).

As a result, this change to a 20-year term will save you $40,000. It will also allow you to be mortgage free 10 years sooner than choosing another 30-year term.

If you need more reasons to reduce your term… you have already paid $53,000. Refinancing for another 30-year term will total $257,800. Plus, you have to add the first five years that you've paid to get to this point. So you've now ended up with a 35-year loan, and are saving only $6,000. And that's not taking your new closing costs into account!

If the time left on your loan is under 20 years, a 15-year term will give you an even lower rate. For anything less than that, most credit unions offer a 10-year fixed loan. After all – the shorter the better – and the quicker you'll become debt free.

Want more information?

The Federal Reserve has one of the best sites for everything you'll ever want to know about refinancing at: www.federalreserve.gov – search for: mortgage refinancing guide.

Identity Theft:
You Don't Need to Be the Next Victim

It was almost like being raped! That was a recent newspaper headline in the story of a young lady who had her wallet stolen out of her car and became a victim of identity theft. Along the way, she was actually investigated for fraud.

This lady was paying for merchandise at a Walmart with her debit card when the cashier advised her that the card was declined. When she called her bank, they asked if she recently opened a new account at another branch? No, she hadn't, but someone had – using her identity. It got worse since the crook had deposited empty envelopes into an ATM machine and had stolen another $10,000 out of her accounts after these phony deposits. The credit bureau wouldn't help her, and even confirmed that a fraud investigation had been launched against her.

When her wallet was stolen four months earlier, she called to cancel her credit cards and obtained a new driver's license. But that was just the beginning of her identity theft nightmare. It was the calls from Esso and Shell, then Sears, collectors for a financed van, and many others, who were calling about items, none of which were hers. She made numerous trips to the police station and banks. All in all, the crooks used her identity for more than $100,000 in fraudulent charges. Eventually, the lenders and banks absorbed the losses, but you have to admit that even a break-in at home would be less frightening, invasive, and time consuming than an identity theft.

Unfortunately, this lady is not alone. More than 12 million Americans become victims of identity theft each year, according to an annual survey by Javelin Strategy. While that figure is staggering, it shouldn't be a surprise that this number will continue to rise rapidly over the coming years.

What are your odds of being a victim?

The largest group of identity theft victims are people under age 25. If that's you, with your social networking and online banking, much of your personal information is online somewhere. You need to look no further than Facebook, where seven out of 10 people share their full birth date, which is a great start (and critical) in gathering enough information for identity theft. At some point in time it becomes a question of *when* you'll face an identity theft, not *if* you'll face it.

Two places where your identity can be stolen rather easily are areas few people think about: your smartphone and LinkedIn. Smartphone owners are one-third more likely to become victims of identity theft. After all, your phone is actually a mini-computer with vast amounts of personal information, and almost two-thirds of people don't even use a password to protect all that data. According to the same study, the networking site LinkedIn has a 10% identity theft rate, which is double the average. Vast numbers of people post way too much personal information on the site, which appears to make it a common go-to place for fraudsters.

If you're a parent of a minor child, your son or daughter is 35 times more likely to be the victim of identity theft before reaching their 18th birthday. In fact, there are more than 140,000 cases of child identity theft each year, according to All Clear ID. In Seattle, a 21-day old baby received a bill for medical expenses from Workers Compensation Claims, and had already been the target of identity theft. The baby, whose only information in the world, was a birth certificate held by the hospital's computers! The reason crooks focus on children is that their identity theft is easier to accomplish, and can be exploited for a much longer period of time. As a parent, you may not even become aware of it until your child is of legal age. Usually the problem comes to light only when your son or daughter applies for a student loan. By that time, the matter is much worse and a nightmare to reverse.

With mounting pressure from parents, Maryland was the first state to pass legislation to help. Effective in January 2013, the Child Identity Lock Bill allows parents to pro-actively freeze their child's credit report. Unfortunately, nobody but you as a parent seems to care. The credit bureaus won't cooperate in freezing your minor child's credit since there isn't an existing credit file. You can put a credit freeze on your minor child's report, but only after an identity theft has occurred. While there are ways around this, you may want to check the web site www.allclearid.com. The free site will scan various data bases to at least provide some clues whether your child's identity may have been fraudulently used already.

On line, the most common way identity theft gets started is through update-request emails. These *urgent* update requests pretend to come from vast numbers of companies ranging from the IRS to banks and brokerage firms. Nationwide, these scams result in over $54 billion in losses, and less than one in 700 is ever investigated.

Data breaches are also one of the first places where your identity theft can start. Over the past few years, companies' card files such as Sony's 77 million credit card files and TJ Maxx's 45 million debit and credit card numbers, are just some of the largest data breaches. In the case of TJ Maxx, it didn't take long for the crooks to use the stolen information to replicate actual credit cards and hit Walmart and Sam's for eight million dollars in gift card purchases. Unfortunately, these thefts have become so common that most people who receive a letter to notify them just tend to ignore them.

However, according to many studies, if you have been part of a data breach, the odds are now 1 in 4 that you'll be the victim of a full blown identity theft. As a result, you cannot simply ignore the notice of a data breach. Go online to the credit bureaus and freeze your credit files as outlined in the credit bureau chapter.

With these types of crimes, however, it is more likely that crooks will simply use your one credit card that has been compromised. It's called account takeover, and it is not the same as identity theft. In these cases, contact your card issuer to dispute the new charges, close the account, and have them issue you a new credit card. Luckily, crooks have nothing more than that card information. As a result, the damage may be minimal, and you are not liable for the fraudulent charges. Account take-over can lead to identity theft if the crooks do have enough additional information.

What makes things worse is that the average person doesn't discover that they have been the victim of identity theft for about 45 days. That's an eternity for crooks who act within the first few days on the assumption they'll be discovered sooner rather than later. However, for the under-25 group, it's almost five months before they find out! By that time, the damage is long done, the crooks have moved on, and all that's left is the nightmare of submitting police reports and disputing charges.

If you want to find out the odds of your identity being stolen, there's a web site that has a questionnaire which scores you from zero chance of identity theft up to 100, and includes tips on how to better protect yourself after each question: www.idsafety.net

If you do become a victim of identity theft, you'll have a new part time job to resolve it. It will take time – a lot of time, as well as energy and costs. Javelin Strategy estimates victims will spend a total of more than $37 billion, or an average $631 per victim.

Studies, and many guess-timates, try to estimate how long it will take you to clean up an identity theft. The most accurate figure is from the Federal Trade Commission who reports that you will spend about 130 hours in getting your credit files corrected and fraudulent accounts removed. That doesn't include the anger, fear, hassle, trauma, or stress you will undergo, as well as the inability to get any type of credit in the interim.

Do you WANT your identity stolen?

Some time ago I was in the United lounge at the Denver airport looking for an hour of peace and quiet. Unfortunately, I ended up three seats down from a man named Walter, and Walter was on a mission. He was on the world's longest phone call to Wells Fargo attempting to get the total interest income on one of his wife's accounts for completing his tax return.

It was obvious from the one side of the conversation that Walter wasn't having much luck. Gee, like he couldn't have guessed that privacy laws don't permit access to someone else's non-joint financial information? But, undeterred, he was not going to be refused.

The first thing Walter shared was his social security number and date of birth. That was just the beginning with what the customer service rep was obviously asking him in order to establish his identity. It was followed by his Wells Fargo credit card number and security code. Becoming more frustrated that he wasn't making any progress, Walter then volunteered his bank account and transit number, telling the rep on the phone (and all of us in the lounge) where his main investments were held. By that time, anyone who was interested, had more than enough to steal his identity, or at least the $50,000 in his investment account, based on the information a frustrated Walter shared with anyone listening.

While you're having a chuckle about Walter's stupidity, think about how much information you share without even being aware of it: not locking down your Facebook privacy settings, not having virus software when you do your online banking, or simply throwing out mail with all kinds of personal information in it.

What will you do?

If you're the victim of identity theft, the first thing you'll need to do is to file a police report. As with other crimes, it legitimizes your claim that any fraudulent charges aren't yours. No matter where you are in the country, or in the world, the crooks used your identity, and federal law allows you to file a police report in your jurisdiction – in your town or city. Without it, nobody will place any credibility in your claim that the charges aren't yours.

> By law, your local police department is required to let you file an identity theft report. If they won't, ask them to read the Identity Theft and Assumption Deterrence Act of 1998 and then file your report.

The second step you should take is to immediately contact all three credit bureaus to place a 90-day fraud alert on your files. As discussed previously, it isn't overly effective, but you'll have done what you can to alert the next creditors who the crooks may target with your ID. Then, get on line and also freeze your credit files. (The contact links to set up your credit freeze are in the Credit Bureau chapter). If you discover your identity theft reasonably quickly, this last step will shut down the crooks from continuing to borrow under your name. If you were paying for credit monitoring and had your identity stolen, you've now seen that these stand-alone programs didn't and can't prevent much of the problem.

You'll be notified after the fact; hence, the reason to set up a proper credit freeze instead.

Unfortunately, there's something else that you probably would rather not think about: a significant amount of identity theft is committed by a family member or friend. Today, without being in the middle of that difficult reality, you should make a decision. If that happens to you, will you file a police report against a family member or friend? Without a police report you're protecting that person and assuming liability for the fraud. It makes you liable for the debt – no matter what. It's a choice. For some it's a very hard choice, for others, fraud is fraud, but it's a decision you'll have to make, should it happen.

Credit monitoring & identity theft protection

Right now, more than 65 million Americans are paying for one of these services or another. Forget the vast majority of companies selling identity theft protection. Stand-alone programs aren't worth the $15 to $30 monthly charge and most can't or won't help you if something does happen. The only program worth having is an integrated plan from a credible company. It has to include an 800 number support network where THEY will spend the huge time, money, and energy getting it fixed with you!

Credit monitoring is a service that's sold by companies ranging from independents to banks to credit card issuers. It's marketed as protection against identity theft and isn't worth any amount of money as a stand-alone service. As far back as 2007, a Consumer Report study found that many of these policies had and continue to have major loopholes in their coverage, guarantees, and insurances. The former well-advertised LifeLock $1 million guarantee, for example, wasn't payable if your identity was stolen; it applied only to defects in their program and set-up. To start your search for a credible credit monitoring service, if the credit monitoring doesn't include access to all three credit reports from the three different agencies, you're not getting the full story.

At least once a month you'll hear of another company or another having their data base breached. As a result, crooks now have another few million pieces of personal information to work with. But not to worry, these companies will always send you a form letter advising you that they'll give you one year of identity theft protection.

Whether it's free, or even worse, if you are paying for stand-alone identity theft protection, it may make you feel better, but it'll do very little to protect you. Many of these services place a 90-day fraud alert on your credit files which they renew every three months. It's something you can do better yourself, and you'll save money in the process. However, this alert is only a heads up note on your file that a creditor should take an extra step or two in order to assure that it is really you who is applying for credit. It generally doesn't happen that the creditor will heed the warning, and with tens of millions of fraud alerts, these file notations tend to just be ignored, assuming they're even noticed. After all, millions of people can only yell 'fire' so often.

The most common identity fraud involves crooks applying for credit under your name and frequently this starts at electronics stores. The crooks apply for instant credit and run up their new card (your new card) for stuff they can easily fence or re-sell, such as computers, televisions, and the like. However, with a credit freeze on your file, fraud artists can't even get started in applying for credit under your name. With that protection, credit monitoring isn't necessary, because crooks can't apply for any credit at all, and are stopped dead in their tracks before they get started.

What fraud alerts are supposed to do in their marketing and advertising does not generally match up with what really happens. For that reason, LifeLock, as one example, paid a $12 million settlement to the Federal Trade Commission and 35 states, alleging that the company made false claims in advertising for their identity theft protection services. They also settled a lawsuit with Experian (one of the credit bureaus), and discontinued offering their fraud alert services.

Almost 12 million adults will fall victim to identity theft in any given year. As a result, these companies who promise to protect you are playing a numbers game. They collect huge amounts of premiums each month and have to pay out only a tiny percentage – if anything at all! In the meantime, millions of people are paying monthly premiums, thinking and hoping that they're protected.

*You cannot simply pay a monthly fee to someone
and hope everything will be OK. Hope and denial
are the worst forms of identity theft protection.*

It's your choice

It is not difficult to take some basic and easy steps to drastically reduce the odds that you will become a victim of identity theft. It's your choice: take the proactive steps or get ready sooner rather than later to deal with the fallout. Hopefully you'll choose the former and mind the following:

- Don't keep your entire life in your wallet or purse. You do not need to have access to every credit card, your social security number, and a bunch of other personal stuff that identity thieves would love to have. Keep as little ID in your wallet as you reasonably need in a normal day.

- Get a shredder and use it. Don't put personal papers or credit card mailings directly into your recycling or garbage.

- Always check your credit card and bank statements for anything strange or unauthorized. You only have 60 days to challenge something, or you own it, owe it, and have to pay it.

- Don't automatically fill in your social security number on every form that asks for it. Challenge the company to give you a legitimate reason why the law requires them to ask. Medical offices, for example, don't need to have it. They only want it in order to assist collection agencies down the road to track you down.

- Don't give anyone your PIN numbers.

- Don't use the same PIN numbers everywhere, and change them every six months or so.

- Never leave any ID in your car – ever.

- Empty your mailbox daily. Some junk mail, and every credit card mailer, contains a lot of personal information. Crooks don't have to do a lot of work, or be extremely bright, to reach into your mailbox.

- Check your credit reports. You are entitled to a free report once a year from each of the three reporting agencies.

- Know your credit card statement dates. If your statement doesn't show up, call the issuer. It may have been re-directed by the crooks.

- Never give out personal information on the phone or in an email.

- Don't click on any email links from anyone. Banks, the IRS, E-bay, Amazon, your investment broker, or anyone else will never ask you to do so. Whatever emails you're getting will be a scam 99% of the time.

Medical identity theft

As crooks get more sophisticated, so does identity theft – and in an area most people would never consider, the medical field. Yes, crooks are actually stealing your identity and using your health-care information for medical procedures.

The odds keep increasing that you may become one of the two million people who fall victim to medical identity theft each year. According to a Ponemon Institute survey, the average fraud has reached more than $22,000. To correct your medical identity theft can also be expensive and time consuming, costing more than $2,000 on average, and taking at least a year to correct. For more than half of all victims, it actually takes more than two years. Money aside, there may also be a lot of pain in reversing what is now a lot of incorrect and fraudulent medical information in your files. That kind of information could get your coverage canceled, future coverage denied, or have other serious implications.

> *"Somebody worked very hard at stealing my social security number and used it to get a job. This has now created a lot of hardship. It has even affected my ability to continue seeing my doctors to be treated for some serious on-going medical problems."* Facebook posting of a friend

How is a medical identity theft even possible? Most medical providers only care that the insurance is valid. Most don't take the time to match it up to the identification of the person who's using it, or take other simple precautions.

When your credit card is fraudulently used, the sophisticated computers of all card issuers catch it much sooner. Their data, and your charges, go through one main clearing house. With medical fraud, you may not notice the problem for an extended period of time, and medical treatments can go to into the hundreds of thousands of dollars.

This identity theft often starts when someone simply uses your identity to get treatment. However, it may be an inside job where someone with access to your medical information sells it to crooks. It's the fasted growing problem area as more and more medical records go online and digital. More sophisticated fraud rings may even set up phony clinics in order to claim payments from insurance carriers using your identity.

As with any other identity theft, follow the basic rules to protect your identity. Remember to get a statement from your insurance company at least once a year to look through your claims history for errors and possible phony charges. If you stop receiving regular correspondence from your provider, contact them immediately as your mailing address may have been changed to avoid detection, and for the crooks to buy some more time.

Some valuable links

To contact the credit bureaus if your identity has been stolen:

TransUnion Fraud Victim Assistance:	800 680 7289
Equifax Automated Fraud Assistance Center:	800 525 6285
Experian:	888 397 3742

Completing your fraud affidavit – the standard FTC fraud affidavit is at: www.ftc.gov – search for: fraud affidavit form.

If you want to calculate your risk level of identity theft: www.myidscore.com.

A great information and resource site from the Consumer Federation of America: www.idtheftinfo.org.

Here is the best website for anything and everything to do with identity theft. This site was started by a couple in San Diego who were among the first victims of identity theft and have been instrumental in leading the nation-wide move for legislation and awareness: www.idtheftcenter.org.

> *It's stupid, it's wrong, but it's true: If you've had your identity stolen, you aren't actually the victim. It's true. The Federal Identity Theft Act states that the victims are defined as those "directly and proximately harmed" by the crime. That includes the credit card companies, retailers, and banks – but not you. The law doesn't consider you the victim and thus, you cannot sue anyone to get help or compensation.*

> *With a one-sentence change, Congress could fix that and help you. But it won't ever happen – the credit reporting agencies would fight that legislation change as it could make them liable for not doing more to help you minimize the damage. Right now, you're forced to rely on law enforcement agencies to investigate. Unfortunately, the agencies often tend to view identity theft as victimless, and your file will rarely become a priority.*

If You're 17 to 21 years old...

If you're between the ages of 17 and 21 (or have a son or daughter around that age group), banks, car dealers, and especially credit card companies, are salivating to meet you.

You're about to graduate and either go into the work force, or start college. Either way, the companies in those industries will do whatever it takes to get your business. Banks, and especially credit card companies, have *the* best marketing minds in the country and want you to be in debt to them – very soon and very deeply.

Almost everyone has an illogically strong emotional attachment to their first credit card. Once the first card is established, the memories and loyalties to this card are way stronger than those of your first boyfriend or girlfriend – and last a whole lot longer.

The average person keeps their first credit card for over 15 years. It doesn't matter that the rate hasn't been competitive for years or that the perks are junk. To be the first in your wallet will make a credit card company a lot of money, for a lot of years. You wouldn't think so, but in your age group, the default rates or percentage of arrears are actually below average. Until you're 21, and unless you have a provable income, your parents will have to co-sign on the credit card. Even if the card is in your name, issuers know that in most cases your parents will step in and pay the balance, or at least make the minimum payments.

Why do they target you and your friends? Because they can't market much to your parents. Adults already have all the credit cards they want, so card companies can't grow their business unless they get to you and everyone else who turns 18. You're one of over four million fresh customers each year, almost all of which can't wait to get a credit card. Also, you don't know much at all about credit and their dangerous traps, but there are good odds that you do love to impulse buy, and you will often be short of money.

The same logic applies to banks wanting to get you hooked on an overdraft or line of credit once you have some income. That overdraft will be there for decades, and it's not like you have the experience to shop around for the best loan deal or most attractive interest rates.

Car dealers also can't wait to meet you either. How many cars are you going to buy in a lifetime? Five, or six, maybe? Well, the average salesman sells that many in a week! So who do you think knows all the tricks and just the right things to say? Who will press your buttons to buy? It's like bringing a plastic knife to a gun fight – you're going to lose, even if you bring one of your parents, or a buddy for support.

So you're all set. You've got your student loan payments for two decades, you've got a credit card, an overdraft, and maybe a car payment if you're in the work force. Grade five math says the majority of your income is now going to pay all of that plus insurance, gas, groceries, rent, and the basics – every single month – perhaps for forever. At that point, if someone tells you to start saving some money, it's almost impossible, just a distant and unrealistic dream.

You may have started thinking about how you are going to get rich in the next 40 years. But you've already forgotten how easy it really is to actually get rich. When you were still in high school you probably had a summer job. You worked hard, had a goal of what you wanted to do with that money, saved like a dog, and paid cash for stuff. Because you had so little money, you were more careful of how you spent it. That was then – this is now. Now you have a paycheck and access to borrowed money, and you're just getting started.

The three keys to financial success are rather simple:

- Pay cash for stuff.

- Don't buy stuff you can't afford and don't need.

- Save at least 10% of your money right off the top from day one, because you can't miss what you don't have.

Out of all the grads from your high school, maybe one or two people will do these. The rest will just be hoping to get rich, or win the lottery. Which group will you be in – the on-track to become financially independent group, or the majority of the permanent 'want be rich' group?

Maybe this short chapter will make you think. Maybe you'll choose to take the steps to becoming a millionaire (see the Graduate as a Millionaire chapter). Maybe you'll choose to want to be financially independent. Perhaps someone who actually cares about your success has made you read this book and this chapter. Maybe you'll see them at the top with you, or maybe you'll be looking for a financial counselor in a decade or so to help you with some of your financial mess…

You're a 17–21 year old who is about to make a lot of financial decisions which will literally impact you for a lifetime. Be careful out there!

"The elevator to the top is out of order – always has been. You're going to need to take the stairs – one step at a time."
Zig Zigler

Graduate as a Millionaire

*Knowing the right thing to do doesn't help
you much if you don't actually do it.*

If you want to be wealthy, the easiest way is to stay out of debt, and to not waste your hard-earned income in payments to everybody. If you can avoid that, you'll actually have money to save and invest.

Could you live on the same small amount of money you had when you were growing up for just another year or two after graduation? Of course you can. But would you, if there was a good reason for delaying going crazy buying and financing stuff for a little longer?

Do you want to make a deal with your parents or with yourself? You can spend every dollar you'll ever make the rest of your life, because you'll already be set to be a millionaire at age 20. The only thing you need to do is to save $10,000 by your 20th birthday, nothing more – nothing less. You can also delay it until age 21, and the results won't be much different. After that, without getting into debt or touching these savings, you can spend every dollar you earn.

It's the magic of compounding interest and works with something called the Rule of 72. It is critical for you to understand this formula and to use it to your advantage, no matter what your age. Simply take the rate of return on your investments and divide it by 72. That's how long it will take for your savings to double. So, at a 7% rate, your money doubles every 10 years (72/7 = 10.3 years), while a 10% return doubles your money every seven years.

Saving that $10,000, investing it, and forgetting about it, even at a 10% rate of return will double your money very quickly:

Investing at age 20:	$ 10,000
At age 27 it doubles to:	$ 20,000
At age 34 it doubles again to:	$ 40,000
At age 41 it's:	$ 80,000
At age 48 it's:	$ 160,000
At age 55 it's:	$ 320,000
At age 62 it's:	$ 640,000
And at retirement (age 67) it's:	$1,280,000

If you have a better, faster, or simpler plan for getting to almost $1.3 million in your investments, everybody would love to know it! Why can't every adult accomplish this later in life? The answer is simply, because they didn't save any money when they were much younger. The longer you wait, the less often your money has to double up, and double up again. If you want the money when you're 65 years old, but only start to save at age 50, these savings will only double a couple of times! In your case, at around age 20, the money has the time horizon to double seven times!

Assuming you want to be financially independent, do some lateral thinking of how you can save $10,000 before you start a lifetime of spending. Becoming a millionaire before you even graduate or work for more than a year or two, THAT is a priceless graduation present and it's not that difficult to achieve.

My favorite coffee place just hired three seniors.
I'd love to know if they're back in the workforce by choice,
or if they had to go back to work. But then, I'm scared
to actually find out the answer…

Relationships and Money:
Before, During, and After

72% of couples under age 30 admit that discussing finances always leads to an argument and 43% hide some of their debts from their partners.
Mint.com survey

Whether it's with your spouse or common-law partner, in any committed relationship, you are more likely to open up about your entire sexual past than to reveal your credit card balance.

In common-law relationships, one partner or another is four times more likely to keep a credit card or savings account from their partner. From a study by creditcards.com, women make up three quarters of this group. In all relationships, Redbook magazine found that 38% of couples lie to their partners about their finances. While those two surveys go back a few years, things have now gotten worse and not better due to the state of the economy, incomes that are barely keeping up with inflation, rising debts, and higher unemployment rates.

While money isn't the root of all evil, as the old saying goes, it definitely has a large impact on strengthening or eroding relationships. Unfortunately, most people often associate money with who they believe they are. Separating bank accounts or going it alone, because it's *my* money, can quickly lead to trouble.

Hiding debts from your partner, with a mindset of, "I didn't tell you, because I knew you wouldn't approve", is not much different from having an affair. After all, the foundation of a successful relationship is trust and doing things together. Owe up to what you owe. Don't let the first few months of your marriage be the start of financial trouble, when bills arrive your partner didn't know you had. Lay your cards on the table. Tell your partner what you owe, way before your wedding day, and way before the bills arrive. You cannot race to the mailbox to hide them for very long.

The most successful relationships, from a financial standpoint, are two people who share a basic financial philosophy and have agreed to common financial goals. These are couples who talk openly, and honestly about money and finances – and always *before* they become a big issue. If not, when the battle lines are drawn, the last comment will usually be a flippant, "well, it's my money!"

Before you get married, you and your partner must agree on money, finance, debt, and savings issues. Agreeing to disagree, talking about it only once, or just keeping your finances separate, are not suitable solutions and will not work for the long term. No successful relationship can start off with a bunch of lies, evading the subject, or choosing to not want to know. Along with the issues of religion, kids, and in-laws, finance and money has to be on the top of your to-do list BEFORE setting a date and saying I do! Until you say "I do", do not combine your accounts or borrow money jointly – for anything – ever. It's a sure-fire recipe for disaster. You are not legally married and should your relationship end, it won't end financially for a very long time. The breakup will become very messy.

Finances and money are the number one cause for divorce, so don't set yourself up for failure before the relationship even gets traction. Not knowing, is not the answer. Way before the wedding, and then at least once every year, sit down with your partner and go through your credit bureau reports. It will let you see each other's entire list of debts. It then starts the discussion of what to do, what to pay off, and how to deal with your financial obligations. If money fights are the number one reason for divorce, wouldn't it make sense to get those issues dealt with in order to boost the odds of your marriage being happy and long-lasting?

If you are married, your attitude towards debt, the use of credit cards, the big-picture savings game-plan, and retirement savings, are not something you can 'mostly' agree on or just avoid. These issues won't magically take care of themselves, and dealing with them some other time will make things worse, not better. While marriage might include being together for richer or poorer, it shouldn't have to be poorer for a lifetime.

The most common problem is often when one partner manages and controls the money and finances. If you're taking care of all the financial decisions, your partner will feel left out, unheard, incompetent, and unvalued. Your partner may not verbalize it, but it's true. This is the biggest reason one partner can often hide debts, or obtain credit cards without their partner's knowledge. It's simply their way of getting some control, or fighting back. If this is an issue in your relationship, look in the mirror and be honest with yourself. Is your financial life a 50–50 deal, or more like 90–10? Even 50–50 doesn't work – those are just the divorce odds! When it comes to your finances, budgeting, spending, savings, and income, it must be 100–100.

When your partner doesn't feel they have input, at some point in time they will go and get the power and control they are missing. However, it may be in destructive ways, and often behind your back. When one partner controls the finances, it's not about their higher math marks in school, they're an ex-banker, smarter than you, or better with online bill payments. Marriage is a partnership. This partnership is a great opportunity to teach your partner, to make him or her feel heard, included, and important. You're not your partner's mom or dad, and not his or her legal guardian.

In addition to the big picture of working together as a team, there are some specific steps that will help your relationship as well as financial situation:

Once as month, have a financial date night to discuss money, your savings, bills, budget, and dreams for the future.

Each of you needs to have a fixed amount of 'me' money each month to spend or to save as you see fit. Whether a manicure is a waste, or lunch at work costs a fortune, it's a choice you make.

Make sure that both of you have a will and that your retirement accounts name your partner as beneficiary.

Establish an agreed-to amount in your emergency savings account. A rough rule of thumb is to have at least three months of your total take-home pay in a separate bank account. Your financial stress and money fights will diminish in direct proportion to the balance in your savings accounts.

Get a proper term life insurance policy to protect your income, which will protect your partner if you were to die.

Agree to a fixed and firm debt-freedom date. It's the date you will be out of debt, excluding your mortgage. When you do get there, your relationship will move to a whole new level. But that's something you won't understand and may not believe until you reach that goal…

If your marriage has ended, if your relationship cannot be saved, you will need to make the difficult transition from feeling with your heart to thinking with your head. At that stage you'll need to deal with the logic and legal aspects of a divorce. Unfortunately, the issues will likely revolve more around debt than actual money.

> *Karen's divorce settlement stated that her ex-husband was liable for their credit card balance and her vehicle payment. That was fine for a year until her ex-husband stopped making the payments. At that point the vehicle was repossessed and the credit card collections started. Karen had no choice but to catch up the arrears and to start making the credit card payments herself.*

A divorce or separation agreement did not take Karen off the hook for her finances. When the credit card was opened, and the vehicle was first financed, she had signed the documents with her ex-husband. Consequently, for better or worse, she was liable for the debt just as much as her ex was. 'He is supposed to pay that', is not a defense and doesn't release her from her financial liabilities. While divorce or separation agreements are also legal documents, the only way for Karen to get her money back is to have her attorney go after her ex-husband for reimbursement.

In order to be fully removed from the liability of any debt, and to protect your credit rating, your name must be removed from all accounts. The lender will need to send you a written confirmation of that. The debt has to be re-financed without your name, by your ex alone. If not, your former partner may continue to pay, and you can hope that it will turn out fine. However, when it may not unfold as it should, by the time you find out there's a problem, your credit score is destroyed and you will be making the payments.

Can You Afford to be a Stay At Home Parent?

In families where both partners work, the notion of one parent staying home to raise the kids is often a goal and a dream. It might not be for everyone, but those who want to do it often feel they can't afford it financially, and the dream dies right there. Yes, almost all couples who have decided to have one partner stay at home, to make raising their kids a priority, will agree that it was hard on them financially. But note that it was hard – in the past tense.

Without doubt, the most challenging steps are in the initial adjustment pains. Can it be done? Yes. Is it worth it? You decide. But just make sure the decision is more about your values, priorities, and family than it is about finances. After all, your credit card companies shouldn't be setting your priorities. In reality, your debts and monthly payments do dictate your life to a one degree or another.

The most common feedback is: "We'd love to be able to, but our family can't possibly make it work without my partner's income." Often however, this *what's-the-use* mindset is not true, because gross income doesn't count. If your partner makes $2,000 a month, you need to deduct the taxes, staff fund, and all the deductions which come off the top, and chances are the real take-home is more likely to be $1,400 tops.

Now subtract the bills which are mostly as a result of earning this second income. If you're like most families, that starts with a second vehicle just to be able to get to work. Are there $300 or $400 in car payments? Then add $200 or so for insurance, gas, and maintenance. What else? Perhaps there are current (or future) daycare expenses of another $400 or more, and probably at least another $100 for lunch, dress clothes, and the like.

Without these 'work bills', the real net income in this example is $400 a month at best, not even taking into account that your working partner may now also move into a lower tax bracket. That's less than twenty bucks a day! Sure, each situation is different, but ten minutes of looking at your finances from a different perspective can have a big impact. It's the old saying: You have to spend money to make money. But in this decision, it totally works against you and makes things worse and not better.

If your desire is to have one partner stay at home, can you really afford not to do it? Yes, it's a one-time adjustment, but if this is something that you really would love to do, it can also create opportunities, bonds, and memories that money just can't buy. So here are a few questions to get you started thinking about the 'how to', instead of the 'can't be done':

- What's the real net pay you're dealing with?

- How much money are you paying out of pocket each month directly related to the job?

- What monthly bills or payments would you be able to drop?

- How much (if any) would your partner's taxable income decrease with only one of you working?

- What bills can you consolidate into a lower payment (or pay off with current savings) to increase your monthly cash-flow?

- Can you get rid of your current car payments by paying off the vehicle, terminating the lease, or trading down to a less expensive vehicle paid in cash?

Today's Problem
Becomes Tomorrow's Nightmare

Unfortunately, most people are better at dealing with a problem when their back is up against the wall, there is a short-term deadline, or the time for procrastination or avoidance is over. It's a very bad idea to delay problems – it's wrong, it's short-term thinking, but it's true and it happens all too often.

In every circumstance, dealing with problems at the last minute, just before they blow up, is also very expensive. When the clock has run out, and the money needs to be there NOW, your available options are directly related to the window of time that's left before something has to be dealt with.

At that point, you and most other people, can make really bad choices, and a minor problem today becomes a financial nightmare down the road. Thinking that you're solving a financial issue today often makes huge trouble for you the following month, or for years to come. Just avoiding some of the following night-mares will make a measurable difference in your stress level and your financial success if you think and plan ahead:

- Paying consumables on credit cards. If you can smoke it, drink it, eat it, or put it in your gas tank, don't charge it. If you don't have a proven track record of paying your credit cards in full every month, what you're consuming, or purchasing today, will require payments over the next several months. Likely, you'll keep charging more of this stuff every week and making things worse and not better.

- Payday loans. Almost two-thirds of payday loans aren't for emergencies, but rather for known bills such as rent, groceries, or utilities. On the 2nd of the month, you'll know you have rent to pay the next month. That isn't a surprise and you have two paychecks before the rent or utility bills are due! On the 30th, you have 12 hours to deal with it, and if you haven't, you're in trouble. On the 2nd of the month you have the whole month to budget, change your priorities, or work overtime to ensure the money is available.

- Paying Visa with MasterCard. If your financial situation necessitates using one credit card to pay another – you're in trouble. Most of the time, the money to pay one, comes from a cash advance off another card. That money comes at a very steep interest rate and pushes you further to the edge of the cliff. Your limit will be reached much sooner and this shell game does have an end. The percentage of your credit limit available for cash advances gets smaller. In addition, you're sending huge danger signals to your card issuer. In a matter of just a few months, these actions may result in having your credit limit cut. The high ratio of balance to limit will also reduce your credit score, which increases your rates and kills the chance of alternate financing.

- Borrowing from your 401(k). About 25% of people borrow money from their own retirement savings. Unless it's a last resort for a legitimate need, with no other options such as an imminent foreclosure, to stop a wage garnishment, or to settle a judgment, don't do it.

The interest on a 401(k) loan is paid to you, but for the time you owe the money, you are losing the potential growth of the investment. Your payments have to be over a maximum of five years, unless it is for the purchase of a home. The significant danger comes if you are to lose your job. At that point, you only have 60-days to pay back the entire balance at a time when you can least afford it. It's no wonder 80% of people caught in that predicament, can't do it. The consequences compound the problem even more as now the entire amount is taxable and will be due with your next income tax payment. At that point, what seemed like a good solution at the time will now have you owing the IRS when there's very little chance you'll be able to pay your taxes in full.

- Cashing in your 401(k). The three most common reasons for you to consider cashing in all or part of a retirement plan are to purchase a home, to cover daily living expenses, or to pay off debts. Let's assume you want to cash in $5,000 to pay off some old bills. The first thing you pay is a 10% penalty right off the top. So you're actually getting $4,500. Then this amount is taxed, as if you made that money as income. Even in just a 25% tax bracket, that's another $1,125. So the bottom line is that the $5,000 you cashed in is really only $3,375 in your pocket.

It gets worse. You may have saved some interest and lessened the financial pressure by paying off these bills, but you no longer have these savings growing and compounding. Here's what you are really out: the $5,000 would have doubled every seven years with a 10% return. Today's $5,000 is $10,000 in seven years, which is $20,000 in 14 years, and $40,000 in 21 years. There was nothing you needed to do but to sit back and watch your investment grow, if you didn't cash it out. The bottom line is that you received $3,375 at a future cost of $40,000, just 21 years from now. It's one of the most expensive ways to get your hands on some money. While it might seem like a good idea today, you are robbing your entire tomorrow to pay for yesterday.

According to the Employee Benefits Research Institute, around 16 million people cash in all or part of their 401(k), averaging $32,000 a withdrawal. What's even worse is that 60% of people aged 20 to 29 do this! The younger you are, the worse the consequences. If you are in your early 50's, the length of time this money should still be compounding and growing is much shorter than it is for someone in their 20's or 30's. It takes years to build up these retirement savings, but only one phone call to wipe it all out...

• Choosing another 30-year refinance. As the mortgage chapter discussed, one of the biggest financial regrets can be your choice of loan terms, especially at the time of a refinance. It'll always be tempting to re-start another 30-year term, and you may not have a choice. If you do have a way to reduce some of your other payments, add some cash to your refi, or change your budget around, you'll be very glad you made the hard choice of not choosing another 30-year term.

A 30-year refi, when you've already paid for a number of years, essentially wipes out most of what you've already paid. Yes, there'll probably be a rate reduction, but the closing costs and extended term will negate most of your savings. Take the time to get the payment options for 25, 20 or 15-year terms, and multiply your payments by the terms. You'll have all your options and the implications of choosing one over another. Besides, how old are you? Add 29-years to *that* figure and decide if by that year you still want to be making some pretty steep loan payments... assuming you didn't refinance yet again after that.

The person who says it cannot be done should not
interrupt the person doing it. Chinese Proverb

Getting From Today to Debt Freedom

A common question is, "what can I do about this or that financial challenge"? But that's not the right question. It should be, "what are you prepared to do"? If you're looking for a shortcut, a quick way out, or a temporary relief of financial stress, these aren't options or solutions to your problems. The quality of your financial life is directly connected to the type of (hard) questions you're prepared to face and answer for yourself.

If you're like almost everyone else in the country, you would love to be debt free. It's not only about the money, but also the feelings, the huge boost to your self-confidence, and how you'll look at the world in a whole different light. Right now, your debts keep you trapped, with very few options, and even less room to maneuver. You worry about a medical problem or the next emergency that can wipe you out, and you keep getting more stressed out at work. That's the life of living on the financial edge. Almost everything has to go right, every day, or you're in real financial trouble. And, if you're like most people, you might be on track to spend your golden years working at the golden arches.

The key question is what are you prepared to do to get from here to there, from living on the financial edge, to becoming financially independent? Wishing and hoping won't make it so, and you do have to put legs to your prayers and steps to your goals. Intentions are great but they don't get anything done.

Commitment is the willingness and discipline to carry out a task long after the mood has passed. Adapted from Josh Huffman

To become wealthy and financially successful in real and meaningful ways can't involve shortcuts. They don't work, as much as you wish they would. It takes hard work, discipline, spending less money than you are earning, saving the money before buying something, and knowing the difference between needs and wants. Unfortunately, the majority of people aren't prepared to do what it takes to become and *stay* wealthy.

> *Achieving your financial goal is way more*
> *about what you're prepared to give up,*
> *versus what you're prepared to do.*

In order to get from where you're currently at to becoming debt-free takes some work, focus, and effort. The main reason you may be in a financial mess is exactly the same reason that the federal government is: they search for quick and painless solutions. In life, nothing worth having is easy – or it wouldn't be so worth it and so satisfying when you reach it. While everyone gets there at different points in their lives, by their own motivators, there are some basic steps that can help you to do more of what works and less of what doesn't.

Stop focusing on getting debt free

Yes, you read that correctly. Rome wasn't built in a day and you can't empty the ocean. You won't run the marathon in two months, but you can go for a 15 minute walk each day. You're not going to quickly lose 40 pounds, but you can lose a pound a week. You also won't be debt free by the end of next month, but you can start on that journey with just one step at a time.

The weight-loss industry generates $61 billion in revenues each year with a failure rate of 95%. That's both staggering and depressing. A large part of the reason is that you're being sold on the theory that it's not really that hard to lose the weight. Nice try.

You may love to hear that the solution is quick and easy, but it's not. Whether it's turning around your finances or losing weight, it's hard, it's a lifestyle change, and it's a lot about saying no to yourself. In an ideal world you'd get seven hours of sleep, drink lots of water, exercise an hour a day, and be debt free. But your world isn't ideal… yet…

> *Actions always speak louder than words. You actually have to take some steps in the right direction. Wishing and hoping to be debt free won't ever get you even one dollar closer. Just like your values need to align with your actions, your behaviors with money and your finances have to align with your goals.*

Why do so few people reach the goal of becoming debt free? Why do 95% of weight loss programs fail? A large reason is that your subconscious mind starts to panic and revolt against that overwhelming goal which seems impossible to reach.

Relax and don't panic by feeling the pressure to become debt free by the end of next month. Do get focused and make it one of your most important priorities, but know the reality that it will take some time. To be successful at anything, you need to stay focused and determined. Never lose track of your ultimate goal, quit on yourself, or look for shortcuts and instant solutions. There will also be times when you have a setback. Stuff – real life – does happen. But what will set you apart from almost everyone else is when you don't let a setback become the end, or where you give up on yourself and quit trying. After all, you cannot have a comeback if you don't overcome the setback. Failure is what you did, and not who you are, and it's never permanent unless you choose it to be!

Persistence pays: Cha Sa-soon is a 68-year old South Korean woman who first started to apply for her driver's license in

the spring of 2005. Step one in South Korea is a 50
question multiple-choice quiz. Just before the end
of 2009, she did it – on her 950th attempt!

You won't get to the end today, but you can take the first steps today. After today, it'll be one day at a time, one small step at a time, which will get you to your goal of becoming financially independent. The goal isn't today – but the first step is today, and every single step is critical and necessary in order to reach your destination. The key is to get going, and to take the small steps that will not overwhelm your subconscious mind into giving up, or create the 'what's the use' mentality.

Don't let your excuses become bigger than your dreams.

Get in sync with your partner

If you're married, you and your partner agreed that it would be for better or worse. Financially, most couples are in the 'worse' situation right now. But when will the 'better' come? What's your game plan for having the better part of your relationship in terms of finances? To be successful with your budgeting or spending and to become debt free, you need to be positively motivated. Not wanting to be broke, or becoming angry that you're paying out your entire income in payments, is a great start to getting your attention on your financial plan. But it won't keep you motivated over the long term. It's also virtually impossible to achieve your financial goals if you and your spouse are not on the same page in sharing similar goals and dreams.

You and your spouse shouldn't stay awake at night
worrying about your finances. You just need to
stay financially disciplined during the day.

There are always two ways you can deal with any issue or decision. You can choose to work on something pro-actively – taking the steps necessary for preventing a problem, and focusing on it before something turns to trouble causing you to hit the proverbial wall. The alternative is to deal with an issue reactively – dealing with the problem after it's blown up, when you have no choice but to make the hard decisions. Unfortunately, most couples end up in the latter category. Is it any wonder that the issues of money and finances are the biggest reasons for fights in a marriage and the highest reasons for divorce? (You should also read the Relationships and Money chapter)

Increase your income

*You own the most reliable ATM in the world: your
ability to earn an almost unlimited amount of income.*

One way to fast-track your goal of debt-freedom is to increase your income. But if you don't get started, you'll never get there. If you currently have $600 a month to pay all of your bills, you can calculate roughly when you'll reach your goal. Yet, if you had $1,200 a month, you'd get there in significantly less than half that time!

If you don't have a PHD (Pappa Has Dough), and you are barely making it from paycheck to paycheck, there's a great place to live: at your job working overtime, or getting a part-time job for a while. Your extra work effort will help you in achieving your goals. And, when you feel the pain of working a large number of extra hours, or the strain of a temporary part time job, it'll be a permanent scar and reminder that you don't want to do that for very long.

While any job will help, and every dollar makes a difference, you should consider taking on a part-time position that you also really enjoy. Any career you love is almost like not working at all. Finding a part-time position in a field that you can be passionate about would be an incredible win-win. For many people, that win-win can come through a home-based business with a professional license. The start-up costs are next to nothing, and a few excellent companies will supply a lifetime of training and support. In those cases, your income can also come with a large number of tax write-offs, ranging from your home office to a partial vehicle expense. You just need to assure that it's a company who is credible, with a long track record, and in a growth industry that you'll want to be with for the long term. If that's so, you'll make it your purpose and passion and quickly transition to it on a full-time basis.

You can't go back in time to make a new start.
But you can start today, to make a brand
new ending to your financial situation
for the rest of your life.

In addition to earning some extra income, you also need to stop taking voluntary pay cuts! Each time you take on a new payment or charge something to your credit card, you're taking a pay cut. After all, that payment now has to be made each and every month, sometimes for years, and it'll come out of your earnings, just like a cut in pay.

To make matters worse, you might confuse your gross income with the real amount of money you get, which is your net pay. Deducted right off the top of your gross income is tax, social security, and other deductions that are out of your control. That reduces your income by at least 25% or so before you ever see the first dollar. From that, you need to make your rent or mortgage payment, pay your utilities, buy groceries, and pay your cell phone, insurance, and other bills which aren't optional either. So when you take your net pay, deduct these necessities (or current living expenses), and what do you have left? There's a good chance that you're down to maybe a few hundred dollars, or you may even be in the hole.

Stop borrowing and buying stuff

There's no chance you can ever earn
more than you want to spend

When you're in a hole, stop digging. The stuff you buy today that you really don't need, takes away the money you needed to pay off the stuff you bought yesterday. And your today borrowing will necessitate payments for the next year, two years, or longer. The most powerful four words to get started on turning your financial life around are four words you're probably not that familiar with: I can't afford it. If you are serious about turning around your financial situation, you will need to practice using that phrase a lot because you're not exempt from the laws of reality.

"Getting by is not the American dream."
Rep. Eric Cantor speech to the A.E.I.

When you decide you want to reach financial independence and become debt free, it needs to start by turning off the buying and borrowing tap, and to end your continuous borrowing and payment cycle. That decision comes with good news and bad news. The good news is that ending your borrowing cycle rapidly accelerates the date of your debt freedom. After all, you've now stopped digging and stopped making things worse. Besides, if you look at all the debt you have, there's a good chance that today, most of it couldn't be sold on e-Bay or given away on Kijiji.

A few years ago, after decades in our family home, my parents could no longer handle the physical upkeep of a large single family home. It turned out that the trauma of selling our family home wasn't nearly as bad as what us 'kids', now middle aged ourselves, had to do in order to make it happen.

One Friday we ordered one of the big commercial dumpster bins to be delivered to the house. After giving away stuff that our family members, friends and neighbors wanted, we knew there'd still be a lot of things that had to be thrown out: sleeping bags to tools, furniture to books, and extra dishes to everything else, none of which could go into a one bedroom nursing home unit. What we weren't prepared for was the visual impact of a huge and full bin being hauled away, then a second bin, and a third bin. In total, the stuff accumulated over a lifetime added up to over 14,000 pounds – in the dump. Few things in life have had such a powerful and visual impact on us.

Literally hundreds of thousands of dollars of stuff, purchased one thing at a time, over a lifetime, boiled down to 14,000 pounds of trash. It sure put things into perspective. You'll now understand why I'm just not that excited about buying that newest whatever, the next model of some gadget or another, or running up my credit cards.

New goals require new behaviors and attitudes to reach those goals. Right now, it's likely that some of your spending habits are pretty engrained, and have been for years. One of the easiest ways to change some of your habits, without getting into a lot of psychological jargon, is to change your routine. Think about the dozens of steps involved when you want to get in your vehicle and drive somewhere. Dozens of steps and hundreds upo77n hundreds of things your brain and muscles are required to do in order to make it happen. They're so automatic with you that you don't think about them at all.

Now watch a teenager who has never driven a vehicle attempt to do that. The process will take ten minutes or more! When you don't have a routine, you don't automatically do things. An inexperienced teenager has to actively think about each and every step, one step at a time. In other words, if you break your routine, you're way more likely to think before just doing, acting, or spending. Which routine do you have that comes with an automatic action for spending? If you constantly overspend and buy stuff you don't need in the grocery store, go with someone who holds you accountable, skip one aisle that makes trouble for you, go to a different store, or go a different time of day, with a specific list, or whatever it takes to get out of your normal habits and routine.

Perhaps eliminate your automatic stop at the coffee place in the morning. Maybe breaking your routine is as simple as leaving five minutes later and taking a different route. You *do* have coffee at work, or you can have another cup at home. If you always go to the mall, stop going to the mall, because you know you end up bringing something home. In fact, the average person going to the mall spends $104 every time they are there! When you no longer have a routine, your brain has to think through each step of what you're doing and it *will* change your behavior. That applies to a diet just as much as a habit such as your spending routine. If you stay in the mode of always doing the same thing, reaching for your wallet is an automatic reaction that you never think about, just like the routine of getting in your vehicle.

What you learned yesterday should show
up in the changes you'll make today.

If you're thinking that won't work, if nothing changes, nothing changes. If you know that you need to take better care of your money you can't accomplish that by doing the same things again and again for another year. Intellectually, you already know that. The question is whether the pain of where you're at is high enough that you're prepared to take in some different information and try something a little differently. Until then your same actions will get you the same results. Or by changing around the words of the Forrest Gump saying:

Life is not like a box of chocolates. It's a jar of jalapenos.
What you do today can burn your butt tomorrow.

Do at least one cash-flow statement

How can you save it or spend it, when you don't
know where it's coming from or going to?

Being broke, overspending, and being way over your head in debt, is not a permanent situation. It's just today's reality. This doesn't need to be a permanent way of life; however, it isn't a one-off incident that got you to this point. It was (or is) a month after month pattern of spending more than you made, whatever the reason or circumstances.

If you're like most people, your pay comes in and immediately gets paid out. Two days after payday, there likely isn't much left in your account. What do you do then? Bring out the credit cards and start another cycle of making things worse? All of your money goes to, 'I don't really know'. If you want to get control of your finances and know what is actually happening with your money, the mindless spending has to stop. There's a lot of your income leaking out to someone, somewhere – all the time. But without a budget, you have no clue where it's going, and without a clue, there's no way it can ever change.

To get control of your finances, you'll need to do something that very few people actually do: you'll need to have a budget in writing. Even the word 'budget', likely has you thinking of a straight-jacket. Instead, think of it as a cash-flow statement. When you see the numbers of where your payments are going, what they add up to, and what's really left over (if anything), it is an incredible reality check. It also makes it much harder to keep denying reality. Denial is a financial strategy. It just isn't one that will last very long. If you don't have a written plan for your money, your money will always find a way to be spent elsewhere.

If it's broken – fix it – don't compensate.

A cash-flow statement is just a snapshot of all income and expenses for one month. It'll immediately allow you to accurately track all of the money coming in and going out in whatever specific categories you choose. Within half an hour you can create a full and complete snapshot of your entire financial life for the past month. It may be depressing, but it'll certainly be eye-opening, and can be an incredible motivator. If nothing else, do this cash-flow statement for just one month. Write down your net income at the top, and then deduct all the bills you have to pay each month. The deductions are your best projection of the money you'll need for groceries, gas, and everything else that you're currently spending. It just takes a blank piece of paper; or, you can google budget forms and you'll find a huge number of sites which have pre-printed and free forms where you can simply fill in the blanks. (There is also a web site link at the end of this section.)

If it's worth it and important enough, we will find a way.
If not, we will find an excuse or a reason not to…

Within a couple of months, you'll be very good at doing accurate budgeting, and will feel totally in control of your money. Information is power, and what you choose to do with that information is up to you. What are you willing to do (or forego) now, so that you can have it all later? Your attitude towards budgeting will have a big impact on your long term financial success. If you (or your partner) believe a budget is designed to handcuff you, you'll fail with your financial plans. You (or your partner) will continue to fight it, by spending beyond the agreements you've made with yourself, or each other. If, however, you go all in, and are committed to knowing it is the only way to proactively control your money, your success is almost guaranteed. If not, would you give it a 100% effort for a 90-day trial period before making your judgment or decision? Make sure that you:

- Keep it flexible. Stuff happens, but that shouldn't affect your overall budget. Be prepared when one expense is higher for the month than you had budgeted. Will you just roll your eyes, shrug your shoulders, and up the budget and pay it? Or, will you force yourself to take that money out of another category because you refuse to increase the total spending for the month?

- Keep an eye on your annual bills. Identify your annual or semi-annual expenses and spread them out over the year. Your budget needs to include one-sixth or one-twelfth of this amount, even if you're not paying it this month. If at all possible, have the money taken out of your bank account and put into a separate savings account each month. If the money is set aside, your budget stays intact.

- Set a cut off amount. Decide on a point, where if you fall below this amount, you will always pay cash. Pick whatever small amount you want, and increase it as you get comfortable with your budget and start to free up extra money each month. All the little $20 expenses quickly add up. When they're charged on a credit card, they're almost impossible to keep track of until your statement arrives. At that point, if the balance is not paid in full, the bottle of wine, snacks, pop, or other consumable expenses are now long gone and you'll be making payments on them for months or years to come.

When I choose to help someone who wants some feedback with their financial nightmare, my first step is to always ask them to send me a budget and their net worth listing. To prepare these takes about half an hour, tops, yet 95% of people who have actually contacted me to get help never even do that simple first step.

The few remaining people almost always spend more than they earn, and it is something they don't even know! Just a quick look through their budget usually shows a couple of items that stand out. One of them tends to be the $150 or so cell phone plan, and the other is a staggering vehicle payment. When I let them know that one or two of those need to go, that normally has most of the rest of the people tuning me out.

So the killer vehicle payments and massive cell phone bills are off the table as far as fixing their financial situation is concerned? If so, what exactly is there left to work with? Were these people expecting some kind of magic solution that didn't involve some sacrifices? How sad that most people won't take the pro-active steps as they're starting to get into trouble, instead of ignoring the problem until there just isn't a good way out anymore.

You're not on this earth to impress other people. In the words of a recent Facebook post, "Ah! The North American way of debt: spending a ton of money I don't have, on things I don't need, to impress people I don't like." There isn't enough money or credit in the world to accomplish that for any length of time. The faster you realize that, the more financially successful you'll become. Practice the four most powerful words, *I can't afford it*, and your self-esteem will not plummet by being broke. The only person you need to impress is yourself, and part of that is accomplished through financial discipline, paying yourself first, and becoming debt free.

One more thing: there are two web sites worth visiting when it comes to planning your budget, becoming more aware of where your money really goes, and what the real price of something is:

Days To Pay lets you enter a few numbers to calculate how long it will actually take you to earn enough money to buy what you are considering: www.daystopay.com.

The second one is a site that will calculate how long it will actually take you to pay for something in full after you've financed it. Or, hopefully, you'll have a look at the total amount before you make the purchase: www.therealdamage.com.

If you're looking for budgeting worksheets you can complete online or print out, one of many is at: www.budgetworksheets.org.

Emergency savings

59% of people could not get by missing one week of pay
National Payroll Association survey

If the above survey result sounds scary, it really is. Almost two-thirds of American adults would be in financial difficulties if they missed one week's pay. In fact, that figure is even higher for young people and single parents. With the national average family income around $49,000, take away 20% or so in taxes, the average net pay a week is really around $800. In other words, an $800 problem or emergency is the difference between serious financial trouble and a minor set-back. Even if you have $800 or so for an emergency, a careerbuilder.com survey had 61% of people admitting that they 'always or usually' live from paycheck to paycheck.

To put you into the rare company of people who are actually able to handle a minor financial disaster necessitates setting up an emergency fund. Whatever it takes, put away one-week of your net pay into a separate savings account. The amount will be different for you than someone else because your expenses and ability to save will also be unique to you. If you make around the average income, the amount will be $700 to $800. It's something most people never have in one account for any length of time. It'll be worth it to you, for your financial peace of mind – no matter what it takes, no matter how long it takes to accumulate it.

> *Your emergency fund cannot be the available*
> *credit remaining on your credit card.*

This money is not for investments and not for the 'emergency' of getting you from the 28th to the end of the month paycheck. It's simply a holding account that will make you not much interest at all, if any. If you cannot trust yourself to leave this money alone, it should not be accessible online or with your ATM card. After that, it's up to you to determine what constitutes a legitimate emergency and has you accessing this money. What you use it for will tell you a lot about your discipline with money and desire to turn around your finances.

Pay off what you owe

*If you don't want to keep starting over
then just quit giving up.*

Debt freedom creates unlimited potential, emotional self-confidence, and a feeling that you cannot imagine until you've been there. No matter what your income is, it'll be all yours, because not a dime is going out to make others rich at your expense. No more worries about missing a week's pay or thoughts of fore-closure. No more credit card payments. No fears that the next phone call might be a collection agency, or the next doctors' visit could wipe you out financially.

After you have your emergency savings, the next and most important step is to start paying off what you owe – the hangover from all those charges and payments. It won't be easy and it won't be quick, but it'll be so worth it. An airliner takes the most amount of fuel to lift off. The largest amount of energy is used to get going, to gain the lift, and to get airborne. The same works for you to get your debts paid off. It'll take a couple of months of focus and extra energy to gain momentum, traction, and a new routine. What it will take is the 2 D's:

The decision – to get started and moving
The discipline – to keep going, to stay on track, and to finish

Do you remember the last time you spilled a cup of coffee or a glass of wine? What did you do? You instantly dropped whatever you were doing in order to clean it up – NOW! Whether you were on the phone, watching a movie, or were running late, nothing else mattered at that time. You got a rag and started cleaning it up, right? The only way you will be successful in cleaning up your finances, debts, and getting control of your money is with that same focus and intensity.

There are two basic ways you can choose to tackle paying off your current debts. Start by identifying the smallest debt or the one with the highest interest rate. Consumer Report actually tested both approaches. They found that there wasn't a significant difference in terms of the interest spent or saved. The only exception would be if you had one debt where the rate is totally crazy and all others are roughly the same.

Whatever you do, you will need to pay more in order to pay less – less in interest for what you still owe. One option is to start attacking the debt with the largest interest rate. While that may seem logical, if it's one of your largest debts, you'll be paying for a year or longer and seeing very little progress in that time. That can seem like an eternity to see much progress. Mathematically it may save you some interest, but often it won't be much. Plus, that small savings you realize will likely cost you a lot more when you reach a 'what's the use' mindset.

The alternate way is to select your smallest bill and tackle it first. It'll create the feeling that you can do it. It's the smallest mountain to climb and it will give you a sense of accomplishment. Make your minimum payments on all the other accounts and dump everything else on the one that you've targeted. Get it set up online and accessible through your ATM. You want to be able to pay lots and pay often. The key is to apply that extra $20 when you have it. Don't put it aside hoping and wishing the money will still be around when next month's statement arrives – chances are it won't be.

Do it today and apply the extra money when you can afford it. It is likely towards a credit card of some kind and they will take whatever you send them and post it to your account. Do it once a month, or five times, it doesn't matter to them. If it's one of your credit cards, the power of paying extra, or just paying more often, is explained in the credit card chapter.

Keep it in front of you. Put the last statement, of whatever bill you're targeting first, on the fridge or tape it to the back door. It needs to always be in your face or it'll be out of sight and out of mind. You want it to be a constant reminder. Every time you make any small payment, write it on the statement and you'll see some really rapid progress.

This is your main focus, and your balance will quickly plummet. Then one day, the balance will be paid off. If you chose the smallest bill, it'll only be a matter of a month or two. However long it may take, keep asking yourself, is it worth it? You bet it is, and you'll become really motivated by actually seeing some progress since it's your smallest debt!

It's OK to dream a little, of what life will be like when these bills are gone for good. What will your stress level be like? What will you be able to save for that you really want, when the hangover of these bills is gone? Freedom is more than just being able to move around, and this REAL financial freedom is just around the corner.

When the first bill is paid off, you can move on to the next. Let's assume you've found a $100 in savings when you did your budget, and you now have a clear sense of your spending habits. Maybe you changed the number of dinners you have out, started being aware of money leaking out each day, or perhaps just started to stretch out the length of time between dry cleaners, haircuts, or other discretionary spending. Just taking this $100 and adding it to your current payments can create some incredible savings.

IF you want or need a boost in your credit score while you're becoming debt free, first get (and keep) all your credit card balances below 50% of your limits. Then go back and re-focus by paying them off one at a time, starting with the smallest one.

IF your focus is solely on getting to be debt free, ignore that option and stay on track.

Step-up debt repayment plan example:

1st bill: Department store card with $800 balance at 21.9%

Your minimum payment at three percent is $24, plus you are adding the $100 budget savings, so you will now be able to pay $124 each month.

Was going to take: 127 months and $920 interest
Now paid off: in 7 months and $59 total interest

Then tackle the next one:

2nd bill: Credit card with $2,000 balance at 19%

The minimum payment at four percent is $80, the amount that you have been paying while focusing on your first bill. That payment has taken the balance down to $1,685 over those seven months costing you $206 in interest. Now you can take the $124 you were paying on the old department store card and add it to the $80 you've been paying here all along, for a new total payment of $204.

Was going to take: 118 months and $1,217 interest
Now paid off: in another 9 months and $341 total interest

3rd bill: Another credit card with $2,400 balance at 19%

On this balance, the minimum payment at four percent started at $96, which you've paid while you were targeting your first two bills. Now it's time to focus on this account in a serious way.

Again, you're adding the $204 from the first two bills on top of the $96 you've been paying, for a total of $300. As you're getting focused on this one, you've already paid $72 for 16 months, so the balance is now $1,623 and has cost $509 in interest. But that's all about to end for this card as well.

Was going to take: 125 months and $1,479 interest
Now paid off: in another 6 months and $597 total interest

You should now already be seeing how quickly extra payments add up. And don't forget, you've only started by adding $100 to these payments. The rest of the savings are from interest and by paying everybody but you, and it gets even better.

4th bill: Vehicle financed (student loan or other fixed loan) of $20,000 at 7%

Hurray! The last target in our example is a loan with a payment of $396. This could be your financed or leased vehicle or any other loan. While focusing on the high interest accounts for 22 months, you've reduced this balance to $13,462 and have paid $2,174 in interest already. Now you're adding the $396 payment to the $300 from the other bills, for a total payment of $696.

Was going to take: 60 months and $3,763 interest
Now paid off: in less than 21 months and $4,055 total interest.

The end result? In this example, you initially had $25,200 in debt, and were on track to pay for 11 years and $7,400 interest. With these changes, it now takes you 43 months – about 3½ years – and you save over $3,300 in interest. What has it cost you? A hundred bucks a month and a little determination!

Follow these steps and you'll be debt free in less than half the time you ever dreamed possible. Want it even faster, with online availability, a lot of professional help, and ongoing support? For a host of reasons, Primerica Financial Services is the one of the only companies in the country that can help you. They've just invested millions of dollars in you, for an integrated, automated program to do the step-up plan with you. If you're ready to become debt free, the details are in the chapter of who to see and who to avoid.

After your debt freedom, life gets better and better, much faster. By now you have taught yourself to take charge of your money instead of giving control to all your lenders and credit card companies. You have $652 extra per month that you were previously paying to everybody else but yourself for the last four years. If you haven't been putting some additional savings aside, maybe this is the perfect time to start. Actually it won't be hard at all since you have the $652 available with no more bills to pay.

You saw what four years accomplished by paying others. Isn't it time for you to pay yourself first? This $652 each month, even at 8.5%, will now grow to over $38,000 in the next four years. That will be your money, which is not paid to any creditors. From over $25,000 in bills to debt-free in less than four years and that same length of time again to create $38,000 in savings, makes an incredible difference – and it all started with a $100 off your budget each month.

Anything you want badly enough in your life, you will accomplish. If you really want to achieve your goals, it'll happen, and a lot quicker than you think. If you need some further motivation, Eric Thomas has a powerful short talk posted on You Tube (search for Eric Thomas – Secrets to Success) that may motivate you.

Who to See and Who to Avoid

*"Impossible is just a big word thrown around by small men
who find it easier to live in the world they've been given
than to explore the power they have to change it.
Impossible is not a fact. It's an opinion. Impossible
is not a declaration. It's a dare. Impossible is potential.
Impossible is temporary. Impossible is nothing."*
Muhammad Ali

One of the most difficult things for most people is to ask for help. If that's you, when you do ask, you'll be amazed at how many people really do want to help. Your odds of success in your financial goals also increases greatly. It's another significant step in reaching your financial goals way sooner than you can accomplish on your own. Yes, at some point in time you'll need some help. It might be with your current debts, insurance choices, or the how and where to start saving some money. But who do you turn to?

The last financial crisis provided ample evidence of the morals and business practices of many big banks, insurance companies, investment firms, and mortgage lenders. The painful financial lessons of others, and some of the insights in this book, have probably got you thinking of the businesses that you may want to avoid:

• Anyone and everyone who uses the word subprime.

• Any company whose advertising is only on payments and doesn't disclose the price.

• Every person or company who mentions the words: whole life, universal life insurance, cash value policy, or annuity. Studies from The Wall Street Journal, many independent researchers, the Consumer Federation of America, and others keep showing that whole life or cash value policies have a below average return and cost upwards of 10 times as much as a term life policy. Walk away. Don't expect the agent to see the light, or to stop hard-selling to get their massive commission. Just walk away – quickly.

You do need to be protected. But it should be a term policy costing a tiny fraction of other policies. The difference is yours to invest, or pay towards your debts. Having the protection is critical – just don't get conned into a bad policy. One-third of households and over 11 million families with kids don't have life insurance of any kind. That's a crisis and not just a problem.

> *I may be out of line, but I don't think so. I have a friend who is now a widow at age 41 with three kids. Previously, as their financial coach, I sat down with this couple three times. Each time they would express how they wanted to get on track financially. Each time I would tell them the first step was to get life insurance to protect their incomes. Each time they would agree, but not carry through. He was making $90,000 a year and had NO coverage. Every time I see her FB posts about what a good a dad he was, and how he loved his kids so much, I get ticked off. Sorry, but he shirked off one of his main responsibilities – to protect his family by protecting his income! Now his family is scrambling for money and is in trouble.   —J.D.*

- You'll probably also want to avoid the major banks. Yes, you'll get the introductory offer and free initial this or that. After that, you'll probably become a number and they'll resume their no-service/don't-care policy. They might be *on* your corner, but they're not *in* your corner. With new regulations, many financial firms are now looking for new revenues. According to the Center for Financial Services Innovation, unbanked or under-banked Americans are a $45 billion untapped market. It's something big banks are now actively pursuing through prepaid cards, check-cashing services, and even short-term payday loans. If there's money to be made, huge amounts of money – from people who can least afford it – you bet the big financial firms will be there. And the bonus for them? Most of these products are exempt from the new financial regulations.

- It's also critical that you avoid the Jones'. Trying to keep up with others is a recipe for trouble and can have you stuck in debt forever. There are hundreds of ways you can practice self-deception. The most common ones include: 'I'm doing better than...,' or 'if so and so can afford it, I can...' Resolve to make your financial life less about image and payments, and more about substance and wealth.

On a positive note, there are businesses that will educate and help you, not sell you. It's always critical to do your own due diligence in choosing who deserves to earn your business. If, or hopefully when, you're ready for some help for the next steps in your financial journey, you may want to start with these:

- Credit Unions have always promoted helping you to save instead of marketing to you to take on more debt. There's a big difference. In Michigan, Credit Unions started a lottery-type savings plan. When you open a savings account, you're entered into a draw for $100 to $1,000 a month, and once a year someone wins $100,000. It's been successful beyond belief. In the first year 16,000 people opened new savings accounts with a total of $30 million. Those savings are the real rewards down the road. Almost 100 million Americans already deal with a credit union, a business that wants to help and even shares profits.

- If you're Hispanic, you also have a powerful ally. One of the best sources of information is the National Council of La Raza (NCLR). It's the largest Latino civil rights and advocacy organization in the country. You can view their website at: www.nclr.org Year after year, NCLR stands head and shoulders above anyone else in keeping the spotlight on discriminatory lending practices. It's almost entirely because of the NCLR that many settlements have been reached and many of discriminatory practices have ended… for the benefit of all minority groups.

- To find a full-service financial firm that you should consider dealing with is more challenging. Yes, there are certainly a number of smaller and regional companies who will actually help you and not sell you. But a small Alabama firm doesn't help you in Wyoming, and small firms usually don't have a long track record, the resources, or even licensing to help anyone from another state. There are solutions; but first, you deserve to read the happier ending of E.M.'s story, started in the credit card chapter:

  > … Over the past couple of years we had looked at a debt consolidation using the house (declined: debt to income too high) and at 0% credit card balance transfers (declined: balances relative to your credit lines too high). We had heard of debt reduction companies and actually contacted one. Their advertising and phone pitch sounded intriguing, but our attorney discouraged us by claiming that most are a scam.

  > Freedom Debt Relief (FDR) appeared to be the answer to our prayers. We enrolled last night! Our plan includes paying off seven credit cards with total balances of $55,327 on which we were making $1,264 payments. We will now be making payments of $754. The $6,000 difference a year is going into savings! At this rate, and reversing the fact that the credit card companies were tanking our credit scores by

lowering our credit lines, we will be YEARS ahead of our initial game plan. We can finally start thinking again about the day we will be able to retire, instead of it just being a pipedream. A heartfelt thanks goes to Primerica – a company that is actually in business to help the consumer get out of debt.   — E.M.

Whether they're already helping you or the family in this story, Primerica Financial Services is one company that stands head and shoulders above others for a number of reasons. Actions should speak louder than words for Primerica. Credibility is measured by what a company does in good times and bad times, even when it's not the most expedient, or the most profitable. For others, just because someone pays money to be on TV does *not* make them credible. It only makes them advertisers.

Because Primerica refuses to do misleading, gimmicky, or any advertising, they need to work harder to make themselves known, in spite of doing the right thing, in the right way, all the time. How sad that credibility can so often be bought by simple advertising. If you're looking for a second opinion, some options, or perhaps a way out, it might be worth your time to get in touch with them.

On their last financial statement, Visa disclosed spending $873 million on marketing. It's not about Visa – all financial firms spend staggering amounts on advertising and marketing. Primerica doesn't do any advertising – period. They work for a cause and not applause. It'd be interesting to know how much Visa invests each year in training and education resources. Pitched and sold versus helped and coached… quite a difference…

Primerica is the largest financial services company in North America with offices in every state, and almost every town and city. In business for almost 40 years, they're a publicly traded company on the New York Stock Exchange (PRI). While they don't say it, their actions clearly show that each of their 100,000 or so licensed representatives knows they will only succeed when you do. They're there whether your goal is to gain an understanding of investment and insurance options, become debt-free, or start a focused savings game plan.

The younger you are, the more critical your financial choices. If you're in your 20s or 30s, most companies don't want your business. Investment firms want nothing to do with you until you have $100,000. Actually, many now require $250,000 for you to get in the door. The focus and help for younger people is what sets Primerica apart from the rest. It's about getting you and young families started with your first $100. It's about getting you to become debt free and helping you to reach $100,000 of investments, instead of turning you away, then sucking up to you once you've reached your financial goals. At that point, it's a little late. Until then, wherever you choose to deal, make sure it's a company that'll actually help you to get educated, motivated, and on track.

Lastly, but most importantly to you, is a new Primerica program called *ENRICH*, which has the potential to revolutionize the financial services industry. The company has just invested millions of dollars to develop the most comprehensive and unrivaled debt elimination program. But it's so much more: it's one place and one focused approach to reaching your financial goals. The membership service includes dozens of features and protections, and there is still more to come. You'll automatically receive your credit report every six months, your real FICO score, and comprehensive credit monitoring. Should you become a victim, their identity theft component will actually have a company work with you in doing what it takes to restore your identity.

Online you'll have your own personalized debt elimination program, similar to the step-up program. The *ENRICH* program is far superior to anything else in that it'll actually get you from: *I should* and *I might* to *I will* and *I did it!* A Primerica representative will actually set up the entire program with you. From adding your accounts and credit cards to the links for automatic bill payments – you'll never be alone, stuck, or overwhelmed.

The second critical feature is that your program is on auto-pilot. Your biggest obstacle of getting from hoping and wishing to reaching your debt freedom is often the discipline and work that's required. No more! This program is entirely automated. It requires only one click for you to track your progress, pay down your debts, check your balances, access your investments, and watch your net worth grow.

The entire financial industry has billions of dollars at stake to keep you naïve, uninformed, and powerless. This Primerica program will change that, and be instrumental in restoring America to financial success one family at a time – starting with you.

It's rare and refreshing to find companies who practice putting their clients first. What a perfect ending to this book – or maybe a perfect beginning for you to have the help and resources to take back financial control, restore your credit, and reach your debt freedom.

Care enough to share:

All the web references and links were accurate
as of the date of printing. If you find one that
isn't working, please care enough to share and it'll
be fixed in subsequent editions. Or, if you find any new
web site that's worth sharing, please let George know at:
www.startfightingback.com or share with others on
Facebook at www.facebook.com/startfightingback